PS8579.U26 M54 2007

Ouchi, Mieko.

Mieko Ouchi : t

2007.

MW01122471

The Blue Light

Mieko Ouchi: Two Plays

The Red Priest

(Eight Ways To Say Goodbye)

Mieko Ouchi: Two Plays

Mieko Ouchi

The Blue Light

The Red Priest
(Eight Ways to Say Goodbye)

160201

Playwrights Canada Press
Toronto • Canada

Playwrights Canada Press
The Canadian Drama Publisher
215 Spadina Avenue, Suite 230, Toronto, Ontario CANADA M5T 2C7
416-703-0013 fax 416-408-3402
orders@playwrightscanada.com • www.playwrightscanada.com

Financial support provided by the taxpayers of Canada and Ontario through the Canada Council for the Arts and the Department of Canadian Heritage through the Book Publishing Industry Development Programme, and the Ontario Arts Council.

Front cover images: Trudie Lee Photography. Top: Kate Hennig. Bottom: Ashley Wright, Mieko Ouchi.
Cover design: Eugene Ouchi
Production Editor: Michael Petrasek

Library and Archives Canada Cataloguing in Publication

Ouchi, Mieko
 Mieko Ouchi : two plays.

Contents: The blue light -- The red priest

ISBN 978-0-88754-520-7

 I. Title.

PS8579.U26M54 2007   C812'.6   C2007-902324-X

First edition: May 2007.
Printed and bound by Canadian Printco at Scarborough, Canada.

Table of Contents

Introduction

In the theatre, what isn't said is as important as what is. Words matter but so do innuendo, gesture, looks, silence; rhythm, noise, darkness, light. The words and everything that isn't the words: both are the playwright's purview, and it is often the unspoken that keeps us in our seats.

Ouchi's words spill luxuriantly down the page in the two plays in this volume. They plunge into the psyches of an unhappy woman in XVIIIth Century France, a professional virtuoso down on his luck, a driven filmmaker on the brink of moral catastrophe. Terrifically playable dialogue tumbles by in scenes both epic and intimate: a violin lesson, a waltz with Goebbels, tea with Adolf Hitler.

But beyond the literary beauty of many passages, for me, the true strength of Ouchi's writing is its profound reserve. "They are in love," a stage direction states laconically in the last few pages of *The Red Priest*—and that's it. The characters never address the subject directly. In fact they barely speak again, and soon they are forever parted.

Ouchi's characters are articulate, active, and brimming with detail and nuance—an actor's playground. But their deeper motives are often barely hinted at. What are the French aristocrat's real feelings for Vivaldi, for music, for being alive? What life circumstances have brought her to this point? In *The Blue Light*, is Leni Riefenstahl monstrously deluded or is she unforgivably deceitful? When the curtain goes down we still don't know. Even such basic information as peoples' names is sometimes withheld: both scripts feature a central character designated merely as "Woman."

In both plays, the precise meaning of certain crucial moments slips away in silence. Take their endings. At the conclusion of *The Red Priest*, The Woman announces "eight ways to say goodbye," but she lists only seven. The eighth is clearly the violin solo that ends the play. But is this wordless goodbye an expression of defiance or of despair, a win or a loss, a leap over the precipice or a heedless crash to the earth? Apologies to Vivaldi who cautions against this very question, but is the final moment of the play happy or sad?

In the last minutes of *The Blue Light*, Leni describes the ideal ending of the movie of her life. It would be a great reckoning; powerful and moving, not inconsequential and unrepentant. But she never says what she'd not be repenting for exactly. Does she feel culpable after all, and if so, for what? She consoles herself with the image of repentance, but never gives voice to any actual, specific remorse. In short, the fundamental thematic questions of each play are vigorously explored but ultimately left for us to answer, after the curtain falls. This makes for very satisfying theatre.

Ouchi's taste for ambiguity and the oblique makes her plays tremendously exciting to work on because they welcome, even demand, the inventiveness of the director, the designers, and the actors to fill in the gaps. This is why they are emphatically works for the theatre rather than literary artifacts. As Festival Dramaturg at Alberta Theatre Projects, where these plays were premiered in 2003 and 2006, it was my privilege to observe director Ron Jenkins' vivid, thrilling *mises-en-scene*, and to witness the beautiful designs and gripping performances Ouchi's words called forth. I have no doubt that other productions will propose very different interpretations—the sign of a good play.

Astonishingly, these are the works of a fairly new playwright. They are Ouchi's first and (basically) her second play. Though so different in setting and scope, they share many themes: the artist as outsider/star; the power of art to transform and to destroy; the personal price of ambition and worldly success; longing and loneliness as the fate of the artist; longing and loneliness as the fate of a woman; a woman's role in a male world—the list goes on.

Will these remain Ouchi's preoccupations as her work evolves? There's no telling, because what's terrific about her as an artist is that she continues to surprise. She's a playwright slash actress slash filmmaker slash artistic director based in a regional centre but with planet-sized artistic aims.

To me, she epitomizes the new generation of Canadian playwright. Though writing from a strongly Canadian perspective, and in her case a female, regional, multi-disciplinary perspective, she fearlessly takes on epic themes, distant places, and long-ago people. She summons form and style and image, and deploys them boldly to suit her particular aims. Then she buries the evidence. Like the Woman in *The Red Priest*, she erases her footsteps, eliminating all sign of herself as she passes. She gives us lots to think about, lots to feel, lots to enjoy. But she also leaves room for her collaborators, especially that most important collaborator, the audience. Room to imagine; to wonder; to "see the world in a different way."

Enjoy.

Vanessa Porteous
Calgary, Alberta, April 2007

The Blue Light

to Vanessa and Ron
for believing in my vision… within reason

*"As if it were a premonition, 'The Blue Light' told of my ultimate fate:
Junta the strange mountain girl, living in a dream world, persecuted
and driven out of society, dies because her ideals are destroyed."*
—Leni Riefenstahl, *A Memoir*

On a project this large, there are many people to thank. To begin
with I would like to thank my parents, my family (especially Kevin
for a place to write in Japan), my friends (especially Brent and Paul
for a place to write in Australia) and Kim for their support of me
during this long writing process. Thanks to all the development
partners including Bob White & Gie Roberts and Alberta Theatre
Projects, John Murrell and the Banff playRites Colony, Marti
Maraden & Lise Ann Johnson and the National Arts Centre & On
the Verge Festival, Vern Thiessen and The Citadel Theatre, and Ron
Jenkins & Jacquie Poissant and Workshop West Theatre. Thanks
also to the long list of artists who worked on various workshops
and readings and on the development along the way: Collin Doyle,
Medina Hahn, Duval Lang, Sandra M. Nicholls, Wayne Paquette
and John Sproule; Patrick Howarth, Ha Neul Kim, Glenn Nelson
and Jeff Page; Dave Clarke, John Kirkpatrick and Gina Puntil; Jerry
Franken, Christian Goutsis, Elinor Holt, Nicola Lipman, Michael
Rubenfeld and Vicki Stroich; Dave Clarke, Jenifer Darbellay, Karen
Fleury, David Fraser, Leif Gilbertson, Natascha Girgis, Dianne
Goodman, Kate Hennig, Trevor Leigh, Duval Lang, Anita Miotti,
Emiko Muraki, Vanessa Porteous, Scott Reid and Rylan Wilkie;
Allie Bailey, April Banigan, Narda McCarroll, Cheryl Millikin and
Georgina Welch.

Special thanks to Alberta Theatre Projects for its incredible
support, and the passion that the whole team at the theatre brought
to the premiere of the play. Special thanks also to Workshop West
Theatre for all of the development support through Springboards,
its beautiful second production and for continuing to be my soft
place to fall. Special, special thanks to Ron Jenkins and Vanessa
Porteous for their vision, their taste, their belief and for being such
incredible creative partners a second time. But most of all, thanks
to the two incredible women who were brave enough to walk in
Leni's shoes a little while with me… Kate Hennig and Sandra
Nicholls.

Leni Riefenstahl holds a perplexing place in my heart. I look at her with admiration, revulsion, reverence and horror. With awe. With dismay.

As artists we will always be judged. By those who are here. By those who come after. By history. By taste. By politics. By hindsight. But there are no easy answers to the questions her life poses.

Because Leni's story is not the hero's journey. It is one of un-repentance. Non-salvation. Un-apology. And a story of how an artist of unforgettable talent gets there.

So I have chosen to shoot her against the sun. And I have chosen to shoot her in the mud. And as Leni accuses, I have made it a lesson.

What that lesson is… is up to you.

—Mieko Ouchi, 2006

The Blue Light premiered at Alberta Theatre Projects in Calgary, Alberta, as part of the Enbridge playRites Festival of New Canadian Plays, February 2, 2006 with the following company:

**THE WOMAN, KARI,
PRODUCTION ASSISTANT,
REPORTER ONE, CHARLOTTE,
PROSECUTOR, PERSONAL ASSISTANT**   Natascha Girgis

LENI RIEFENSTAHL   Kate Hennig

**FATHER, ADOLF HITLER, WALT DISNEY,
REPORTER TWO**   Duval Lang

DR. FANCK, GOEBBELS, CAMERAMAN   Trevor Leigh

**HANS "FLEA" SCHNEEBERGER, THEO,
HEINZ, REPORTER THREE, JUDGE,
EDITING ASSISTANT, PHOTOGRAPHER**   Rylan Wilkie

Director	Ron Jenkins
Set & Props Designer	Scott Reid
Costume Designer	Jenifer Darbellay
Lighting Designer	David Fraser
Composer & Sound Designer	Dave Clarke
Sound Designer	Leif Gilbertson
Production Dramaturg	Vanessa Porteous
Choreographer	Anita Miotti
Stage Manager	Dianne Goodman
Assistant Stage Manager	Karen Fleury
University of Calgary Intern	Emiko Muraki

The Blue Light was first commissioned and developed by the National Arts Centre English Theatre (Ottawa).

The play received further development assistance from:

Alberta Theatre Projects
The Banff playRites Colony—a partnership between the Canada Council for the Arts, The Banff Centre and Alberta Theatre Projects
The Citadel Theatre
The National Arts Centre and the On The Verge Festival
Workshop West Theatre

═══ ACT I ═══

A black stage. Slowly, creeping, a cold blue light begins to illuminate the stage and we gradually see the form of an old woman. She is waiting.

A slight breeze from God knows where, blows her hair back. She breathes it in. Shift.

She begins to move slowly. Years melt off. It becomes a dance. She is suddenly and surprisingly wild, uncontrollable, mesmerizing. Young again. Dancing in the style of choreographers Mary Wigman and Isadora Duncan, natural and passionate.

She dances a brief and representational version of the story of The Blue Light. *A young girl is drawn to a mountain by a mysterious blue light. She climbs towards it, sleepwalking. She reaches the top and looks into her beloved cave of crystals. The cave is empty. They're all gone. She teeters for one long sustained agonizing moment.*

She collapses.

WOMAN *(entering)* Miss Riefenstahl…

She pronounces it "Rife-in-shtall."

Miss Riefenstahl? Oh God…

She rushes over to the crumpled figure. Light reveals they are in the office of a Los Angeles film studio executive. Spare and minimalist.

Here.

The WOMAN helps her to sit. Hands her a Kleenex.

Are you okay?—

LENI —mnnn.

WOMAN Are you sure?

LENI Yes.

WOMAN *(not convinced)* I'll get you some water—

LENI   —I don't *need* water.

It's just very hot in here. You should put in some air conditioning. I thought you Americans loved your, how do you call it… canned air?

WOMAN   We have— *(changes her mind)* I'm sorry Miss Riefenstahl.

Pause.

LENI   *(getting it together, taking in the WOMAN, the office)* You kept me waiting for quite a while.

WOMAN   It's been a crazy week. These days we're making trailers for films that haven't been cast yet…

LENI   You kept me waiting in this… stuffy room for quite a while. Your assistant—

WOMAN   —Peter—

LENI   —whatever… he said you wouldn't be long.

WOMAN   I'm sorry… Like I said, it's been a crazy—

LENI   —If I were a big-time producer, I wouldn't keep filmmakers waiting.

A challenge.

WOMAN   I'm a little hot as well…. Let me get us both some water.

She leaves. LENI slumps a little. Then pulls herself back together. The WOMAN quickly reappears with two bottles of water.

Here you go…

Stubborn, LENI doesn't take it.

LENI   Can we get down to business?

WOMAN   Of course.

She sits behind her desk. All business.

When Peter said that you had sent us a script, I was surprised.

LENI   Really?

WOMAN   Well, Miss Riefenstahl, I—

LENI   —Ms.

WOMAN   *Ms.* Riefenstahl.

LENI   *(correcting) Reef*-in-stahl.

>   *Pause.*

WOMAN   I was surprised to receive your script. But intrigued.

LENI   You knew who I was?

WOMAN   Yes...

LENI   You knew my work?

WOMAN   Of course.

LENI   You seem awfully young to have this job.

>   *LENI stands unsteadily. The WOMAN stifles the urge to assist.*

WOMAN   ...I'm afraid I'm not as young as I look.

LENI   Ah yes, of course... Los Angeles...

>   *She walks around the office, checking it out. It's huge.*

WOMAN   So... this script. It's unusual for us.

LENI   What do you mean?

WOMAN   Well, we don't get pitches like yours through the door every day. It was a treat to read such a literate pitch.

LENI   You don't find filmmakers want to make literate films these days?

WOMAN   Well... sure they *want* to. Every young filmmaker with one indie feature under his or her belt wants to do a modern "adaptation" of some classic for their Oscar bid. I get ten of those a day. But I swear, half of them haven't even read the original... whatever... they're wanting to adapt. They're basing it all on vague memories of some 700-page novel they were forced to skim in a high school English class—

LENI   —I see.

> *Pause.*

WOMAN   But anyway… your film.

> I have to tell you, I personally would love to see this film made. It's a fascinating story… Amazons… it's virtually untouched territory…

LENI   Did you know her story before?

> *Letting her off the hook.*

> Penthesilea?

WOMAN   She's real?

LENI   Well, I suppose that's up for debate. She's a "character" in *The Odyssey*.

> Homer… yes?

WOMAN   Right. So… how did you come across it?

LENI   I was forced to skim it in high school.

WOMAN   Ah.

LENI   Well? Give it to me straight. What do you think? Is it a go?

WOMAN   Well… it would be premature to say anything that definite.

LENI   Your boss. Do you think you can convince him?

WOMAN   *(She laughs.)* Well that's not really necessary… I… well I don't have a boss…. But that doesn't mean I can green light whatever I want. Distributors… Shareholders…. It would be a hard sell. If it had a boy coming of age, or fly-fishing or…. Well that's a whole other battle. Have you brought this to anyone else?

LENI   Yes. I have.

WOMAN   Because it really does harken back to a time when films were—

LENI   —Everyone else.

Pause.

WOMAN   This city can be a little cold.

Takes a chance.

I don't know if I should tell you this... but... ...I wrote a paper about you in film school...

LENI looks at her.

(emboldened) So... I know it's been hard since—

LENI   —Since what?

WOMAN   Well... since... since the War.

LENI   I don't know what you're talking about.

WOMAN   I know you haven't made another...

LENI   I'm a photographer.

WOMAN   Well, yes, I know—

LENI   —You *know*? You know what?

WOMAN   Well... I know you never—

LENI   —never what?

WOMAN   Made another film.

Pause.

LENI   Well contrary to what you might think, that was my choice.

WOMAN   Oh.

LENI   I've had opportunities to, but for many reasons, I decided not to.

WOMAN   I see.

But now...?

LENI   Now I want to make one. This one.

Pause. The WOMAN isn't sure how to respond.

I know what you're thinking.

She's old, ancient practically; she can't possibly make another film. She won't make it to the end of production. She won't make it to the end of *prepping* for production. Shit, she might not make it to a second draft.

WOMAN   Of course not.

LENI   Oh please. Admit it. You're thinking this old lady's what? Almost 100? This is crazy…

WOMAN   No…

LENI   What about Wilder? He was no spring chicken. Look at Huston. John Huston? He was practically dead when he made that film, what was it—the last one? "The Dead"?

WOMAN   Well that's a little different.

LENI   How?

WOMAN   I don't know. They were making films and—

LENI   —One day *they* were dead.

>   *Pause.*

But I'm different.

WOMAN   *(admitting)* You're… different.

LENI   Why? Because I didn't keep making films?

WOMAN   Because…

LENI   Ah…. Because I chose to be a *photographer*.

>   *The WOMAN doesn't say anything.*

Right.

I don't know why I bothered. It will never end—

WOMAN   —I'm sorry—

LENI   —until I'm dead…

>   *She stands and grabs her coat and purse off the back of the chair. She teeters briefly, and then suddenly falls.*

WOMAN   Oh…

>   *Is she dead?*

Oh God!

FANCK   Cut! Brilliant, Leni!

> *Shift. To reveal LENI being filmed by an intense looking man, Dr. Arnold FANCK, and his cameraman, Hans "FLEA" Schneeberger. LENI is young again, athletic and vibrant. She is at the height of her film stardom. 1926. Twenty-four years old. On the set of "The White Hell of Pitz Pallu." FANCK is instantly besieged by questions by his rather sparse crew. The WOMAN crosses to LENI, worried.*

WOMAN   Are you all right?

LENI   Shit. Fine.

FLEA   *(helping her up)* Jesus… you all right?

LENI   *Ya, ya, ya…*

> *The WOMAN is still gawking at LENI. She has become a young production assistant.*

FANCK   *(to her)* What are you staring at? Make yourself useful, for Christ's sake!

ASSISTANT   Yes, Dr. Fanck.

FANCK   Prepare for the avalanche!

> *The WOMAN exits. FANCK crosses back to his crew.*

FLEA   "Brilliant Leni!" …Must be nice.

LENI   What? Are you jealous?

FLEA   I never hear "Flea, I know we just threw the lead actress off a cliff on top of you and you not only survived this, but you managed to keep the camera rolling for this *single take* creating some of the most incredible near death footage never seen on film before. Brilliant Flea!"

LENI   *(laughing)* What are you implying?

FLEA   Nothing… I'm just saying, this makes the Great War seem more and more like a vacation every day…

LENI   Maybe we should trade. I'll shoot and you can play my part. Maria, poor stranded newlywed forced to survive in the wild…

She poses dramatically.

"White Hell" is right…

FLEA   I wouldn't wish that storyline on my worst enemy.

LENI   What do you expect? Arnold's a geologist, not a filmmaker.

FLEA   *Ya*, well, a year ago I was a skier, not a cinematographer.

LENI   And I'm a dancer, no actress…

FLEA   Please… *(quietly)* He's lucky to have you…

FLEA smiles at her. A moment. FANCK sees.

FANCK   Flea?

FLEA   *Ya, ya, ya…* *(to her)* Got to go play God… re-light the Arctic…

He joins FANCK and goes back to work. LENI watches him leave. Looks out over the mountain pass. Shift.

LENI   I remember the first time. The first time I felt your lure. I was standing on the platform, waiting for a train in Berlin to see a doctor. An injured dancer. The ultimate cruelty. Out of the corner of my eye. A poster. The film was called "Mountain of Destiny." By Dr. Arnold Fanck. I don't know what possessed me. I suppose I wanted to lose myself. See something magical and mysterious and the mountains seemed to be all that to me. Hold all that. And in that split second, I left the platform and walked in.

I had always thought of the cinema as cheap entertainment. Theatre had always seemed so much more refined. Cultured. Expensive. Father always said the cinema was for people who couldn't afford the theatre. Poor people who couldn't afford the clothes. The tickets. The dinner beforehand. The drinks after.

But that day, I took my place among the rough, unwashed men. The shabbily dressed women. And I was struck, as I sat there among the silent, expectant rows, how familiar they were. That they waited for the film to start like my childhood congregation waiting for Sunday Mass.

When we got up to leave, I was a changed person. I felt ashamed for what my father had said. For what he had made me imagine. For what he had made me believe.

And I knew what I had to do.

I had found my church.

>   *Shift.*

FATHER   *(hard)* Leni!

LENI   Yes, Father?

>   *LENI is suddenly eleven years old. Her parent's house, 1913.*

FATHER   Stop daydreaming.

>   *He's packing. He lays out the rules.*

LENI   Yes, Father.

FATHER   You must be a good girl while I'm gone.

LENI   Yes, Father.

FATHER   And you must mind your mother. You must listen to her and be obedient.

LENI   Yes, Father.

FATHER   And you must do your studies.

LENI   Yes, Father.

FATHER   No more mooning about dancing when you should be at your books.

LENI   But, Father—

FATHER   —Leni, I won't hear any more about it.

>   And you must listen to your brother.

LENI   But, Father, Heinz is only eight—

FATHER   —Heinz is the man of the house, while I'm away.

LENI   Yes, Father.

FATHER   And do your chores.

LENI   Yes, Father.

FATHER   And not be scared at night if you hear sounds.

LENI   Yes, Father.

FATHER   And you must hug your old father.

LENI   Yes, Father.

> *She gives him a small obedient hug. He doesn't let go.*

FATHER   *(a shift, suddenly gentler)* And tell him how much you love him.

LENI   *(surprised)* Ya, Father.

> *She hugs him more tightly. A real hug.*

FATHER   And promise not to miss him too much.

LENI   *(tiny)* Ya…

FATHER   He'll be back soon.

LENI   *Ya, Father.*

FATHER   *(Disengaging and picking up his suitcase, he takes one long last look at her. Stern again.)* Goodbye, Leni. *Auf Wiedersehen.*

> *He leaves. She watches him go. She is surprised by his unexpected affection. Her face crumples. FLEA and FANCK roll by on a dolly pushed by the crew. Filming "Storm Over Mont Blanc," 1930. Shift.*

FANCK   Cut!

LENI   Shit…

FANCK   Back to firsts! We're going again!

LENI   What was wrong with that take? I almost cried didn't I? Jesus—

FANCK —we're going again!

>And less melodramatically this time. She's a young woman, a child nearly… innocent and naïve about the world.

LENI What do you think I was playing?

FANCK You're playing her like a bitter old crone.

LENI This script makes me *feel* like a bitter old crone. It's obvious what this scene is about—

FANCK —who's directing this film? You or me?

>*Silence. A stand-off.*

LENI You.

FANCK Exactly. Now, we're going again.

FLEA *(breaking in)* Arnold, there's a shadow back there. I'm sure its driving you as crazy as me…. Take a break and I'll get one of the boys to put a flag up…

>*Long pause. FANCK and LENI haven't broken their stare.*

FANCK Break everyone!

>*FANCK exits.*

FLEA *(knowing what's coming)* Save it, Leni. You're wasting your breath.

LENI He's lost his mind. Sure he can trigger an avalanche on people, Flea. That doesn't take talent. That takes stupidity. Film after film, he sticks us on a mountain with a flimsy plot. The only difference between any of them is the title… what's this one? "Storm Over Mont Blanc"? No wonder I'm losing my mind, I'm making the same goddamn film over and over again! But you know what the real tragedy is? He can't see what's right in front of him. What he *used* to understand. The real power of this place. Not just a place to shoot these ridiculous melodramatic adventure stories. But moments of magic. Myths. Dreams.

>*Abruptly, he kisses her. A long passionate kiss. LENI breaks it off. Gets up.*

I have to warm up—

FLEA   —Leni…

LENI   What?

FLEA   It's just you were so angry and—

LENI   —I'm stiff—

FLEA   —and passionate and—

LENI   —and I've got to get ready—

FLEA   —you're the only one that has the guts to stand up to him—

LENI   —Flea—

FLEA   —that's what I love about you.

> *A moment. She looks at him.*

LENI   I'm an actress remember? People think I sleep with everyone on the set already. All they need is fuel for the fire.

FLEA   People don't care, Leni…

LENI   I've heard that before—

FLEA   —I swear—

LENI   —just to see it plastered over all the newspapers in Berlin the next day. My mother crying, hiding the papers from my father, wondering if I'm pregnant and alone holed up in some hotel.

FLEA   You wouldn't be alone.

> *Pause.*

I mean. If you were to get pregnant. You wouldn't be alone. I would be there. I mean, I would marry you. Well… I would marry you even if you weren't pregnant but…

LENI   Stop talking.

> *LENI kisses him. Passionately. Long.*

FLEA   Leni…

LENI   It looks like Arnold is good for something after all…

> *They laugh and kiss again. FLEA picks her up and spins her around. Shift. As they come around the final time, she has become old. Slumped and limp in his arms. FLEA has become a young man, THEO. The summer intern. The WOMAN is there, holding a clipboard, a package and a jacket.*

WOMAN   Jesus… I don't know what happened. She was fine…

Here.

> *The WOMAN helps him set LENI down in an office chair. Slumped, eyes shut, she doesn't move.*

THEO   Should I call an ambulance?

WOMAN   No. Fuck. No…. That's all I need.

Thanks for your help. What's your name?

THEO   Theo.

WOMAN   Of course. Theo. You work for…

> *He nods.*

Right…

> *He takes his jacket and package from her. Hands her back the package.*

Right.

> *Hands her the clipboard. She signs for it.*

Theo you've been very helpful. My… …grandmother isn't feeling well, and she does this every once in a while. She just needs to lie down… The thing is, she's very embarrassed about her fainting spells, so if you could keep this to yourself that would be great.

And you know Peter… Peter, my… …yeah…

> *He has been staring at LENI. He nods.*

If you run into him at the cafeteria, could you send him over? That would be great.

He looks back at LENI lying there. Concern. Not sure if he should leave.

I really need him. If you could just find him and send him over.

She shakes his hand. He takes one last look at LENI and leaves.

WOMAN   Fuck… fuck… FUCK!

A hundred fucking years old and she comes to *my* office and fuck…

She goes over and stares at her. Nothing. She leans over to get a better look. Nothing.

Shit!

Miss Riefenstahl? Can you hear me? You passed out but you're okay now…. Fuck.

Can you hear me?

Nothing.

Miss Riefenstahl?

Miss Riefenstahl?

Miss Riefenstahl?

LENI   *(very quietly)* Ms…

WOMAN   What?

LENI   *(louder)* Ms. Riefenstahl.

WOMAN   You scared the shit out of me.

LENI   Ya… I've been told that before.

Pause. LENI slowly opens her eyes. Takes in her surroundings, tries to sit up. The WOMAN helps her.

WOMAN   Are you okay?

LENI   *(shaking her off)* I'm fine!

WOMAN   Jesus, why are you so—

LENI   —What?

WOMAN   I'm trying to help you.

LENI   Go to hell.

WOMAN   Why are you mad at me? I'm trying to help you.

LENI   Go have your lunch. Go have your meeting. Just leave me here—

WOMAN   —I'm not going to leave you here—

LENI   —why not? What do you care? I'm just an old lady—

WOMAN   —of course you're not…

LENI   Yes I am. An old lady with a script about *Amazons*—

WOMAN   —No you're not. You're fucking Leni Riefenstahl.

LENI   Aha…

That's what you're so afraid of. That's what's got you hopping around with bottles of water and Kleenex…

WOMAN   What?

LENI   Don't want to go down in the history books as the woman who killed Leni Riefenstahl.

WOMAN   No!

LENI   Believe me, there are lots of people who would thank you.

WOMAN   *(gathering herself)* Look, I don't know what you *imagine* I think of you. But I just want to say for the record, I don't hate you. I'm not sitting here judging you.

Yes, I know who you are. But I also know, what happened, was a long time ago…

LENI   Not long enough.

WOMAN   You made films during a time of… well… it was a complex time…

Pause. LENI stares at her.

LENI   What self-important little undergraduate history class did you get that from?

Did you write that down? Did you think to yourself, yes, I'll remember that. That will sum it up. "It was a complex time…"

LENI picks up steam.

The problem with young people like you…. No, the problem with young *women* like you is that you think you understand. You feel *compassion for*. You *identify with*. Me.

You probably feel you have something in common with me because you've struggled too, am I right? To have a career in the film "industry" as you young people like to call it these days. Oh… you write papers about me. You defend me in film studies class when you hit that chapter called "Propaganda"… Am I wrong?

The WOMAN stares at her, says nothing.

Of course not.

You think you're so unique?

She struggles to rise.

Well you're not so unique. You've all seen me. You've all snuck me in the back door. Every one of you young women with your big desks and big jobs. Every last one of you.

WOMAN   So why are you here then?

LENI   I'm a filmmaker.

WOMAN   Well, in that case, you may have seen a hundred of me, but I've seen a *thousand* of you.

Beat.

LENI   Really.

*Shift. We are instantly on the set of "The Blue Light,"
1932.*

It starts like a dream.

The arches of the grotto light behind her like a church.
LENI is transformed into JUNTA. They are on the set of
"The Blue Light." The WOMAN disappears.

A book opens to reveal its story. A story about a mountain.
And a mysterious small mountain village. In it,
a young girl, Junta, lives as a pariah. Rocks thrown at her
for being odd and mute. Chased down the streets. The
townspeople believe she's a witch. Barefoot and in rags,
she runs and hides on the mountain, taking sanctuary in
her own world.

One fateful night, a full moon illuminates the peak.
Asleep, the young girl answers a call like none she has
ever heard before. The call of the mountain itself. A call
coming deep from its heart. The Blue Light. Sleepwalking,
she climbs barefoot, up steep rock faces and cliffs, and
across crevasses where other people, other men from the
village, have fallen to their death. But she's different. She
climbs effortlessly. The mountain chooses to show her his
glassy path to the pinnacle. There, he reveals his true
nature. His true secret. A cave. A cave of crystals, which
only visible in the blue light of the full moon, take her
breath away.

> *With that, we realise that FLEA is silently shooting her, the*
> *camera on a tripod. She stares out at the crystals before her*
> *for a long moment. Kneels. She reaches out for one and*
> *picks it up trembling. A magical moment.*

(*a whisper*) Cut…

> *Pause. She looks up.*

Well?

What was that? I'm not sure I heard you—

FLEA   —you were right. It's a better shot.

LENI   No, it's better than better. …Flea?

FLEA   It's beautiful.

LENI   No. Stunning.

FLEA   *Ya*, I'm stunned. Who knew you'd turn out to be such a good actress?

> *She laughs.*

LENI   Actress? I'm the *director* now remember?

FLEA   *Ya*—

LENI   —A director who *against* the wishes of her cinematographer, decided to re-shoot—

FLEA   —*ya, ya, ya*—

LENI   —and created a better, no a beautiful… no… a *stunning* shot.

FLEA   Don't be cocky Leni, I was around *before* you were a director, remember?

LENI   *Ya*, well, look where we are now.

FLEA   What? Alone on a freezing set, on the side of a mountain, in the middle of the night? What the hell's changed?

LENI   Flea, no more shitty adventure films. No more Arnold screaming at us. We can finally run our set the way we want to. *Shoot* the way we want to. Even in the middle of the night if we want to. Like tonight. I got an idea. We came out here—

FLEA   —and that's an improvement? Well, you're quieter than Arnold. I'll give you that.

Nicer to look at too…

> *He kisses her.*

LENI   *(breaking away)* You know, what we've shot with the red filters, it's turned out so beautifully. Now we need close shots of the crystals to match. Everything else we shot of the grotto, I'm going to throw out. It's wrong, too sharp, harsh—

FLEA   —Leni—

LENI   —and I've been thinking, for the tight shot of the crystals, I want to try flaring the lens. I know you *cine-*

matographers don't like flares, but I was thinking we could use it, on purpose, as a transition—

FLEA —Leni—

LENI —Flea, let's get these shots, and we're done—

FLEA —I don't want to be done.

> *She looks at him.*

LENI You want to stay out here all night?

FLEA Leni, don't do that.

LENI What?

FLEA You're shooting this film like… …Arnold.

LENI *(hurt)* What the hell is that supposed to mean—?

FLEA —we've been shooting day and night. No one can catch their breath, let alone take in what we're actually doing…

If this film really is about the search for beauty… the way you've been trying to convince us it is? Why can't you just stop for a minute, on the side of a mountain at midnight, in a grotto of crystals, and enjoy one little moment with me?

> *LENI has no response to this.*

Jesus, you're so far ahead of yourself, you're not even here.

LENI Flea? I want to get those last shots… I need them for editing.

> *No response from him.*

Flea. I *want* those last shots. Now.

> *He turns and looks at her. Long pause. He gets up and crosses back to the camera.*

(lightly, trying to make up) I don't see why you're making such a big deal out of this. I *am* enjoying this moment.

I just have to get this film done. If I can prove to them I can do this, that I'm a real director, there are people out there who will support us…. There'll be more films. More moments like this. With more money, we'll have more time.

> *FLEA turns and looks at her.*

FLEA   You're so naïve.

LENI   Flea—

FLEA   —Listen to me. Savour it, Leni. You can't always recapture the magic of the first time.

> *They stare at each other. A stand-off. He goes back to the camera and starts to shoot the crystals. LENI watches him. We slowly build back into the "The Blue Light."*

LENI   But, someone sees her that night. A man. In awe, he watches her climb the mountain that killed so many others. He falls in love with this wild, primal girl; climbing with her bare hands and feet. He follows her, placing his heavy booted feet in the map her small bare ones left in the snow. As they climb the treacherous path, he begins to wonder if the rumours about her being a witch are true.

But as he crawls exhausted onto the final plateau, he sees at last, that she has not led him astray. To his death. She has led him to a cave. A holy church of ice and snow.

> *FANCK appears. Coat and hat on. Shift.*

> *The magic is gone. Months later.*

FANCK   I got your message.

Flea.

> *Stepping out from behind the camera.*

FLEA   Hello, Arnold.

FANCK   As it turns out, I do have some time…. So, I took the train.

> *Pause. LENI says nothing.*

But I have to get back soon. So… are you going to show me this mess you've put together?

FLEA   *(seeing LENI's face, jumping in)* —The Steenbeck's down the hall. The rough cut is on the plates…

FANCK   Harder than you thought… eh Leni?

She looks at him.

Pretty shots are only the start. Editing is about revealing the heart of your story.

He goes to leave. Turns back.

When you calm down, come find me. I'll show you how to cut your film.

He exits.

LENI   Godammit… dammit!

FLEA   Leni, we agreed—

LENI   —that doesn't mean I like it—

FLEA   —How many years has he been doing this?

LENI   I know. I just… I hate his fucking films.

FLEA   You need him. Editing isn't a skill you can just pick up over coffee in a morning—

LENI   —Yes, I realize *that*.

FLEA   Well then?

LENI   I thought I would be able to do it.

FLEA   Just like you thought you'd be able to climb a mountain without a lesson?

LENI   *(hurt) You* had no experience when you first picked up a camera.

And anyhow, I climbed it, didn't I?

FLEA   So what do we do Leni? I don't see any way around it. The rough cut is a mess. Just let Arnold help you make sense of it—

LENI   —"The Blue Light" is my fucking film…

FLEA   Then do what's best for it. Swallow your pride. Let him cut it.

> *He exits. LENI stands for a moment alone. A well-dressed man steps through the door. Watches her for a moment.*

GOEBBELS   Good afternoon, Miss Riefenstahl.

> *LENI is caught off guard. Shift. Dr. GOEBBELS's office. 1932.*

LENI   Dr. Goebbels.

GOEBBELS   Thank you for coming. I hope I didn't keep you waiting too long.

> *He strides into the room, his office, to his desk.*

Kari… could you get us some coffee please?

> *The WOMAN looks at LENI. Then exits.*

I trust coffee is agreeable with you?

LENI   Yes.

GOEBBELS   I think coffee is nice late in the afternoon.

Of course the British like their *tea* around this time of day, but we don't want to emulate them, now do we? *(laughs)* We shall have some good strong coffee instead.

Please… sit down.

> *She does. He sits at his desk. Sizes her up.*

Well, well, well… Miss Riefenstahl.

An actress.

LENI   Yes.

GOEBBELS   A dancer.

LENI   Yes.

GOEBBELS   An athlete.

LENI   Well…

GOEBBELS   Skier, climber…

LENI   … *ya* I suppose…

GOEBBELS   And now… perhaps a filmmaker.

LENI   I hope so.

> *Pause.*

GOEBBELS   I saw you, you know, in "The Blue Light."

Unfortunate. The title, I mean. So close to that other film. I imagine it's pretty difficult to go head to head with *her* star these days.

> *He glances at her. No reaction.*

Ah well, timing aside, not to worry, Miss Riefenstahl. Miss Dietrich may have garnered all the accolades for that mannish performance, but I think I can truthfully say… I liked your film much, much better.

> *He considers her. Smiles.*

You know my mother used to tell that folk tale to me when I was a boy. *The Blue Flower* yes? I recognized it immediately.

When I was little, well… probably like you, I always imagined that magical cave of light my mother described… and you captured it beautifully. It was just as I envisioned it. It's been so many years since my mother told me that story. But it's funny how clearly I remembered it. Your film brought that back.

It is a powerful story.

A good story for us all to remember don't you think? Especially during these times. These hard times we live in now? If you think about it, in so many ways, we are like Junta, that young innocent girl you played in "The Blue Light." Misunderstood. Living in misery. Surrounded by jealousy. Like her, we must protect our own little crystals no? Here in Germany? Our own jewels? Or else one day we may go to our cave like Junta and find them all gone.

> *LENI looks at him.*

But I bore you with talk of politics…

You know, I must admit, I've enjoyed your work for years. So daring. So athletic. Always. I wasn't sure what to expect in this film, this film you directed, but I immediately saw you have vision. Confidence as a director. And seeing you now, I realize how completely you transformed yourself for the role of Junta. You were… how can I put it in words? Well… different than you were in your other films most certainly. Not just powerful, but primal. Primitive…

KARI enters with coffee on a tray.

Ah… I think you will enjoy this.

She places the tray on the table.

LENI   Thank you.

> *KARI whispers in his ear. Hands him a note. He reads it. He nods at her.*

GOEBBELS   *(rising)* I'm sorry to cut our meeting short Miss Riefenstahl. But something has come up. You understand?

LENI   Of course.

GOEBBELS   I trust that we will be able to work well together.

> *He holds out his hand. She is surprised. KARI shoots her a look. They shake hands.*

Until our next meeting. *Auf Wiedersehen.*

> *He's gone. LENI is not sure what has just happened. KARI follows after him, taking one last look at LENI as she exits.*

HEINZ   Leni?

> *Shift.*

LENI   Heinz?

HEINZ   Hello, big sister.

> *HEINZ, her brother, appears. In a uniform. LENI sees him and runs to him.*

LENI   Heinz! What are you doing here?

Buries her head in his chest. She is 21 years old. He is 18 years old.

HEINZ   Leni! Leni, don't be so silly.... Why are you always so melodramatic? I've only been gone a month—

LENI   —it feels longer.

HEINZ   Don't be ridiculous. And I wrote you, didn't you get my letters?

LENI   *Ya.*

HEINZ   And didn't you read them?

LENI   *Ya.*

HEINZ   Well?

LENI   Don't go back.

HEINZ   Leni, you're talking nonsense. Don't you listen to Father? *(imitating FATHER, stern)* "There is *nothing* more commendable for young men than training as an officer. It builds character. Discipline. Obedience."...

(confides) Besides... it's fun.

LENI looks at him.

Well it is! It's this or sitting all day in Father's office...

She feels his coat. The uniform is brand new.

...nice eh? A little big, but Momma's cooking should take care of that...

I almost forgot. I brought something for you.

He pulls a trinket out of his pocket. Black metal. Mechanical. Almost gun-like.

LENI   *(scared)* What is it?

HEINZ   What do you think? A toy, silly. You turn this handle and a little picture plays. Look in here.

He points to a tiny eyepiece. She looks into it. HEINZ turns the small handle on the side.

LENI   Ah!

HEINZ   Can you see the horse?

LENI   *Ya!*

HEINZ   Well, there you go. When you get lonely or worry, silly girl, you can look at this and watch his legs go around and think of me and old Max, galloping with the others.

> *He gets out a smoke and lights it. Watches her cranking it over and over.*

Have you been all right, Leni?

LENI   Mn mn…

HEINZ   Momma?

LENI   Mn mn…

HEINZ   Father?

> *LENI nods.*

Where is he?

LENI   Shed.

HEINZ   …still puttering around that damn shed…

I guess I should tell him I'm home. He'll want to hear the full report of what we've been doing.

> *He doesn't want to go. LENI looks at him.*

But then again… I could just stay here and look for Leni…

> *LENI starts to laugh and runs and hides.*

Where did she go? I swear I just saw her…

> *HEINZ pretends to look for her. Their old game.*

(*pretending to answer FATHER's question from outside*) Leni?

I don't know, Father! I can't find her.

> *LENI steps out from her hiding place and watches him. He doesn't see her. Magical shift.*

LENI   Beloved brother.

HEINZ   *(to her hiding place, he still doesn't see her)* Father says, "You're to stop your damn dancing and do your damn chores." I don't know how you do it, Leni, staying here, you're stronger than me.

> *Nothing. He smiles.*

Hide away, Leni, I won't tell…

FATHER   *(off)* Heinz?

HEINZ   Coming—

> *He exits. She crosses to the window. She watches him go out to the shed. She looks down at the camera still in her hands. She runs it.*

LENI   One single horse.

> One single horse with his legs going round and round. One single horse with one single man. One little favour. One tiny request. One single horse. One single man. One single horse with one single man…

> *Watches the tiny movie again and again.*

GOEBBELS   What is that?

> *She starts. Shift. She is in GOEBBELS's office once again. She has been waiting. He stands in the door. 1933.*

LENI   *(putting it away)* Nothing. A silly toy…

GOEBBELS   May I see…?

LENI   Of course… Dr. Goebbels.

> *She hands it over.*

GOEBBELS   How does it work?

LENI   Um… you hold it up to the light like this… and look in there…

GOEBBELS   How clever.

LENI   And turn this.

GOEBBELS   Ah… I see. The horse running… of course.

> *The moment has become oddly intimate.*

What a very special thing. You must treasure it…

LENI   Well… it's just something they made to show people how films worked, I suppose.

GOEBBELS   I guess it worked.

LENI looks at him.

Please.

He indicates the chair. A fresh start.

Thank you for coming to see me today. I've been thinking about you since we last met. Since we had coffee that day. You made a very strong impression on me.

And I'm not the only one.

Our Führer received the letter you sent him.

He unfolds it with a snap, and we are instantly transported to the moment he first read it. Shift.

Dear Herr Hitler,

"Recently I attended a political rally for the first time in my life. You were giving a speech at the Sports Palace and I must confess that I was so impressed by you and by the enthusiasm of the spectators that I would like to meet you personally.

LENI pulls out her own copy of the letter with a snap, and is instantly transported to the moment just after she has written it. She reads what she has just written. Shift.

LENI   Unfortunately, I have to leave Germany in the next few days to make a film in Greenland so a meeting with you prior to my departure will scarcely be possible: nor indeed do I know whether this letter will ever reach you. I would be very glad to receive an answer from you."

In their own realities.

BOTH   Cordially,

Leni Riefenstahl.

Snap back to the scene. GOEBBELS continues.

GOEBBELS   It was bold to send such a letter, audacious even, to ask for a meeting…

But, like myself, our Führer was charmed by your passion. He was sincerely pleased, I think, that you were so moved by his speech at the rally.

You should know. He's seen your film. And liked it very much. The premise intrigued him. Like you, he is dedicated and keen to make sure our German stories are told and remembered.

So, after we spoke, I had a thought. I see a chance, an opportunity perhaps, well… how to put this? I am in charge of the *Reichfilmkammer*, yes, but I am no artist. I don't pretend to be.

But you are.

I believe you can help the Führer express himself, his thoughts and his feelings to the people of Germany. His pride, his love of this country and his passionate desire to show the world, that we are a force to be reckoned with. Not a country that can be shoved around and treated without respect as the rest of Europe would have us.

Like the Führer, you expressed so much of what we are trying to do for the German people with "The Blue Light," but not with the heart of a politician. With the heart of an artist.

Do you understand?

LENI   I would make a film.

GOEBBELS   Yes.

        Pause.

LENI   With you.

GOEBBELS   Yes.

        Pause.

LENI   And I would direct the film?

GOEBBELS   Yes.

LENI And write the film?

GOEBBELS Yes.

> *He smiles.*

LENI I would have control over the film.

GOEBBELS Well, yes. *(He laughs.)* Within reason. As I have said, I'm no artist. My arena is politics. I would trust the artistic vision to you.

LENI You would allow me to do what I wanted?

GOEBBELS *(enjoying this)* Yes. Within reason.

LENI …And the finances?

GOEBBELS Taken care of.

LENI Crew?

GOEBBELS Whomever you want.

LENI Distribution?

GOEBBELS *(laughing)* Well, yes!

> *Pause.*

LENI Why me?

GOEBBELS What do you mean?

LENI Why not Fanck, Pabst or… well anyone else? They have more experience. More skill.

> *Pause.*

GOEBBELS I like *your* film.

That's all.

LENI That's all.

GOEBBELS And, perhaps like Junta, I want to look at my beautiful cave one more time.

> *Beat. He takes a sip of his coffee.*

We would like you to film the next rally that the Führer speaks at. We want to capture the power of his live speech.

The power that got you to sit down and write this letter. The power that got you to walk to the post box with this letter, and against your better judgment, mail it.

We need to capture that command. That authority. That passion. On film. So that even people who aren't able to see him speak in person, understand him. Can hear his message. Consider this a test.

> *Pause.*

LENI   What about the editing?

GOEBBELS   The editing?

LENI   *Ya.* Who will edit?

> *Pause. He considers her. He pours himself another coffee.*

GOEBBELS   Well, I hadn't really thought that far in advance. Is that important?

LENI   To me it is. I believe it's where you find the heart of the film.

GOEBBELS   And *you* would like to edit?

LENI   Yes. I would.

GOEBBELS   Well, then… I suppose that could be negotiated.

LENI   Negotiated?

GOEBBELS   Depending on how things go. Yes?

> *He looks at her.*

WOMAN   I need to say I'm sorry. For some of the things I said earlier. I was out of line.

> *LENI turns. The WOMAN is standing, looking at her.*

I've been on this side of the desk so long; I forget sometimes how hard this process is for filmmakers.

LENI   Yes.

> *Confused, she turns back. GOEBBELS has disappeared, but the feeling lingers. Shift. Back to the present.*

WOMAN   So… let's talk about your film. *(reading off her script)* "Penthesilea."

You've been working on it for a while?

LENI   Oh no… not long. Only since 1939.

WOMAN   Right.

> *Uncomfortable pause. LENI lets her off the hook.*

LENI   Actually, I've had it in my mind even longer than that.

WOMAN   Really?

LENI   I was on a train, on my way to do my very first film as an actress. I had just finished my supper when I heard a voice say: "Penthesilea—at last I've found my Penthesilea."

WOMAN   Who was it?

LENI   Max Reinhardt. And here he was, a great director, waving his napkin and telling me that he had a dream of creating the dance of Penthesilea and that I was the one to do it.

WOMAN   And?

LENI   Well, of course he didn't know about my injury. And it was bad timing. I was off to make a *film…* and that just seemed so much more exciting…

But somewhere in the back of my mind, his words always stayed with me.

WOMAN   You obviously really connect to her story, to keep working on it for so long, to come here and pitch like this.

LENI   What? You mean to risk humiliation? By pitching to a woman, a third my age?

WOMAN   I guess.

> *LENI laughs.*

LENI   I guess you have my answer then.

> *She looks her over.*

Will you accept some advice from an *old* woman?

Beat. The WOMAN nods.

Life plays a mean trick on us all. This lovely period where everyone who needs and wants something from you, is older than you? When you are *wunderkind*? When you have power *and* youth? You'll soon discover this lovely period only lasts a delicious brief moment. You'll be surprised how quickly you'll join the ranks of the old, the written off and the over and done with.

WOMAN   You're talking to someone who makes films for tweenies. Believe me, I understand we all go out of style.

LENI   Out of style? That will become the least of your problems.

How about out of time.

Pause.

WOMAN   Will you accept some advice from a younger woman?

LENI   *(laughs)* Sure. Bring it on… as you say in L.A.

WOMAN   Okay…

What the hell… I'm just going to say it.

If you really want to make another film… why not just apologize publicly once and for all for your involvement with the Nazi Party?

All it would take is showing some remorse.

LENI   Remorse.

Pause.

Remorse for what? How the world turned out?

WOMAN   Well no—

LENI   —so they can re-vision me?

WOMAN   No—

LENI   —revise me? Rehabilitate me?

WOMAN   No.

LENI   So they can give me a lifetime achievement award and pat themselves on the back for being so goddamn open-minded?

WOMAN   People want you to take responsibility for what you did. To publicly say that you worked with Hitler and you were wrong.

LENI   You make it sound like I was a policy-maker. I'm sorry to burst your bubble. I'm a *film*-maker. I just made films.

WOMAN   But you didn't just make films. You made *propaganda* films.

LENI   I made documentaries.

WOMAN   For the Third Reich.

Whatever you want to call them, the films you made helped further the cause of fascism—

LENI   —well if that is your standard, isn't every film a propaganda film?

Doesn't every film further a cause?

WOMAN   That's different—

LENI   —what about this Michael Moore you're all so in love with, and his so-called documentaries. You think what he's doing is without an agenda? That it's not furthering a cause? You all just let that go by because he's on the so-called left. Because he's selling what *you* think.

Pause.

Did you really feel so good watching him skewer an old man with Alzheimer's?

Even if it was Charlton Heston?

How will history judge *him*?

WOMAN   People were leaving Germany. You must have had a sense at least. You were in the inner circle.

LENI I wasn't friends with him. I made documentaries for him. You of all people must understand that.

WOMAN What do you mean?

LENI Your studio—

WOMAN —don't. I know what you're doing—

LENI —do you believe in every film they make? That you produce? Would you stake your personal reputation on every single one of them?

WOMAN No. Of course not.

LENI And your head CEO, are you held accountable for his decisions? Are you held accountable for the decisions of your studio's subsidiaries? The beer companies? The newspapers? The television networks?

WOMAN That's different.

LENI Really?

WOMAN They're not fascists.

LENI As a filmmaker, I can tell you that's debatable.

I wouldn't be so cocky sitting at your big desk. You don't always see it coming.

> *Shift. LENI's editing suite. She is in the middle of cutting. GOEBBELS appears behind her. July 1933.*

GOEBBELS Leni—

LENI *(exasperated)* —What now?

> *She turns.*

HITLER Miss Riefenstahl.

LENI *Mein* Führer.

> *She is shocked. She salutes.*

HITLER Please…

Don't be angry with Dr. Goebbels. I've made him interrupt you when you have much to do, I'm afraid. I won't take up much of your time, but I wanted to stop by and thank you in person.

LENI   *Mein* Führer.

> *He studies her.*

HITLER   It was a little disconcerting to see you and your cameraman, shooting well... everywhere... at this last rally, but nevertheless, I am very pleased you have agreed to assist Dr. Goebbels and myself.

LENI   *Mein* Führer.

HITLER   Please. It is my honour to work with you. "The Blue Light" was a remarkable film. I hope it is a foreshadowing of what you will create for us.

GOEBBELS   As I was saying, we're almost done editing "Victory of Faith" *Mein* Führer, but it is a very humble film. A test really. A rehearsal. We are in the midst of much more elaborate planning for the filming of the next rally, *Mein* Führer.

HITLER   Nuremberg?

GOEBBELS   *(nodding)* We hope to do something much more spectacular.

Show the Führer your plans, Leni.

> *They both look at her expectantly. She pulls out blueprints of the square and nervously spreads them out.*

LENI   I would like to shoot this rally in a new way. A different way. Well, I am *hoping* to...

> *HITLER says nothing. LENI hands him some of her storyboards.*

I don't just want to record you speaking. I want to show the effect you have on the people.

HITLER   The way it affected you, Miss Riefenstahl?

LENI   *(surprised)* Yes. The way it affected me, *Mein* Führer.

HITLER   I see...

She looks at him carefully.

LENI   But to make a film like this. It will require some changes.

Pause. He looks at her.

HITLER   Changes?

LENI   Well, changes in how they enter the square. The soldiers, I mean. And the flags. And the way they file in. The way they are lined up.

GOEBBELS   *Mein* Führer I—

HITLER   —let her speak.

I would like to hear her reasoning for why I should re-order the entire armed wing of the Third Reich.

Long pause. LENI gathers her courage.

LENI   *Mein* Führer, it is simply that the camera sees things differently than they exist in real life. It makes no logical sense I know, but sometimes when you film things as they really are, they lose their power.

He is skeptical.

HITLER   I see.

LENI   When I'm directing a film I need to manoeuvre things, rearrange things, manipulate them even, to create the images I want, the feelings I want, even though it looks odd in real life.

HITLER   But the final product looks right.

LENI   Yes, *Mein* Führer.

HITLER   Powerful.

LENI   Yes, *Mein* Führer.

He looks at her for a long moment. The tension is thick. Finally he smiles.

HITLER   Kind of like a painting.

LENI   *(surprised)* Yes.

HITLER   I know this is on a much different scale… but when I paint, I sometimes have to do the same thing. I remove things that don't work. Add in small details that strengthen its power.

I see why your films are so strong.

I don't care how odd it looks in real life. I want the rally to work as a film.

LENI   *Mein* Führer.

HITLER   We have a deal then. I will take care of the speech. You take care of the cameras.

> *He goes to leave.*

Miss Riefenstahl, please let Dr. Goebbels know if there's anything else I can do to assist you.

GOEBBELS/LENI   *Heil* Hitler.

> *He exits.*

GOEBBELS   You're a better actress than even *I* thought.

LENI   *(turning on him)* Why didn't you warn me?

GOEBBELS   What?

LENI   Why didn't you tell me he was coming?

GOEBBELS   What are you talking about?

LENI   Don't ever do that to me again. Don't ever show up like that.

GOEBBELS   You think I had a choice?

> *She puts the blueprints and storyboards away.*

Leni, you have no idea what I've done for you.

Now be nice and accept my apology.

LENI   No.

GOEBBELS   Leni, let me make it up to you.

> *He tries to take her hand.*

LENI   No.

GOEBBELS   Leni… come on. I'll do anything.

LENI   No!

GOEBBELS   Leni, please—

LENI   —all right.

I don't want this film to be produced just by the Ministry.

He stops smiling.

I want it to be a co-production with me.

Pause.

GOEBBELS   My little Junta grows wings.

LENI   I want to prove to them, I'm not just an actress.

GOEBBELS   You're a director.

LENI   A producer.

GOEBBELS   An editor.

LENI   A *filmmaker.*

Pause.

(a test) You said you'd do anything. Will you do that for me?

Pause.

GOEBBELS   Yes. Yes I will.

You shall have your own film company. Just like Fanck and Pabst and all the rest, Leni Riefenstahl. I'll see to it myself.

He kisses her. He goes to exit.

LENI   I have one more request.

I have a brother.

Pause.

GOEBBELS   Ah… I think I understand. Your brother serves the Führer doesn't he?

And now you want a medal for him? To make your father proud? You're a good sister.

He goes to kiss her. She evades. She can't bring herself to ask.

LENI   …Not a medal…

A pardon. An honourable discharge.

GOEBBELS   There is no honourable discharge. Serving Germany and the Führer is the greatest honour a man could have.

Becoming harder.

Or a woman for that matter. You overstep your place to ask that for your brother.

Holds her hard by the shoulders. Looks her in the eye.

Don't push your luck little bird. Like the Führer said. We have a deal. You'll have your film company, Leni Riefenstahl, but the film had better be brilliant.

He kisses her. Hard. A threat. He releases her and exits. She stands alone for a moment.

FLEA   Leni?

FLEA stands in the doorway.

LENI   Flea?

Shift. She turns and runs into his arms. Holds him. Safety.

Oh God. I'm so glad you came. You have no idea what this has been like—

He gently but firmly untangles himself. He looks at her.

What? Don't look at me like that. God I look a mess I know, I've been working around the clock… I've been trying to get ready.

What?

What's wrong?

FLEA   I…

LENI   What?

FLEA   I can't work on this film.

LENI   But Flea you have to. I need you. We've done everything together. It will be "The Blue Light" all over again. Only better. So much better. I can see it in my mind. I'll get you out of any other obligations you have. I can do that now—

FLEA   —It's not that.

LENI   God, you're not still…

        We've talked about this. We both agreed it was for the best—

FLEA   —It's not that, Leni…

LENI   What then?

FLEA   I won't work on this film.

LENI   Why?

FLEA   Because of him.

LENI   Josef? He's all right. Look, he's better than Fanck. He doesn't care that I'm a woman. He believes in my talent, he trusts my vision. Finally, I've got what we always dreamed of. We've got our backing—

FLEA   —Not Goebbels.

        She looks at him.

LENI   What?

FLEA   Hitler.

        Pause.

LENI   *(quieter)* What are you saying?

FLEA   I won't make a film for him.

LENI   The Führer?

FLEA   Yes.

LENI   Flea, don't—

FLEA   —Leni, listen to me!

LENI   Don't say another word.

FLEA   Why?

LENI   You don't know…

FLEA   Are you afraid?

LENI   No—

FLEA   —Yes you are…

LENI   No—

FLEA   —Yes you are! Because it *is* dangerous.

LENI   No!

FLEA   You feel it because it's there, Leni. Danger.

LENI   Let go of me.

>   *She pulls away. Turns from him.*

FLEA   You're playing with fire. And you can't just turn a blind eye. You know what people are saying. About him. About him and you—

LENI   —how dare you—

FLEA   —you've heard what he's saying. What he's proposing—

LENI   —no.

FLEA   People are leaving. Lang. Pabst. Dietrich. Why?—

LENI   —I don't want to hear it—

FLEA   —don't lie to yourself—

LENI   —what he says has nothing to do with me. I'm an artist, not a politician.

FLEA   You are an artist, Leni. Don't let them use you.

>   *She slaps him across the face. He stares at her for a long moment. He turns to go.*

LENI   You're just like the rest. You're jealous. You're just jealous that he chose me. Not you. You're just like Fanck. Like all the rest of them. To you I'll always be an actress, a girlfriend, a mistress… not a real director.

He leaves.

I don't need you. I don't need any of you. I'll do it myself!

*Shift. She slowly turns to the audience. Hard. Cold.
HITLER appears. We are at the rally.*

I unleashed a wave upon them.

I unleashed a tsunami of perfect rows. Flawless. Vicious.
Holy. The SS and SA were re-organized into the clean lines
I had originally envisioned. I ordered them to do it, and
they did what I told them. They did exactly what I told
them. I lined up the flags. The banners. Every last one of
them. Just as I saw it in my dreams. The boots. The hands.
The sky.

I cast the parts of the ecstatic congregation myself. The old
peasant woman weeping with patriotic love. The young
boy drumming and chanting with the zeal of a disciple,
worship shining in his eyes. And Hitler himself. I placed
him, as if at a pulpit. On my knees, in the dirt, I shot him
against a sky set ablaze with light from the sacred shrine
of Germany. Pious. Powerful. Invoking God himself.

I designed and directed every frame. I rode the dolly.
I framed the shots.

For better or for worse, it's mine.

For better or for worse, I made my film brilliant. And
perfect.

And…

…unforgivable.

Blackout.

End of Act I

═══ ACT II ═══

*The present. The office. LENI stands looking out the
window, lost in thought. The WOMAN sits staring at her.
LENI sees her expression.*

LENI   (*confused*) Where were we?

WOMAN   Fascism. You just called me, and the studio I work
for, fascists.

LENI   Ah. Right.

Pause.

Have you ever made a film?

WOMAN   Why?

LENI   I'm just curious.

WOMAN   Is that the rule? Like those who teach, can't? Does
every film executive have to be a washed up filmmaker?

LENI   You tell me.

Pause.

WOMAN   I made some shorts and I made one feature.

LENI   What was it about?

WOMAN   My feature?

Why are we suddenly talking about my failed filmmaking
career?

LENI   Ah… failed…

WOMAN   Not technically failed. I got distribution. People saw
it. Well, some people… why does this matter? Why are we
talking about me?

LENI   I guess I just want to know where you stand.

WOMAN   I don't stand anywhere. I made some films. Now
I don't. I hear pitches. I pick the ones I think I can get
through the system and actually get made. It's as simple
as that.

LENI   It's never as simple as that.

Beat.

WOMAN   You're right; nothing is as simple as that.

The WOMAN considers her a moment.

You could make another film, you could change everything… if you just apologized.

LENI   What do people want from me? To apologize for being
born?

WOMAN   They want you to admit that at the time, you put
your career ahead of what you probably damn well
guessed was going on—

LENI   —ah here it comes—

WOMAN   —to admit that you made those decisions—

LENI   —what you've been waiting to say all morning—

WOMAN   —because you wanted to make films. You wanted to
be a filmmaker. It's ugly, but isn't that the truth?

LENI   No.

WOMAN   Really.

LENI   No.

WOMAN   Believe it or not, I think people would understand.
Especially in this town.

I mean, haven't we evolved as a society? Maybe we've
finally come out the other side of colonialism, slavery and
internment… to something else… whatever you want to
call it…. Redress, mediation…. Truth and Reconciliation.
We understand your decision because it's human. We all
make decisions we regret. That we later know were
wrong.

LENI   Wrong. I see. And what exactly is wrong with my films?
My *documentaries* you studied at film school? If they're so
wrong, why did you study them?

Oh yes, right. Because the years they were made, people
said they were the best films in the world. Because there
was nothing wrong with them. Just because society has

---

evolved as you put it, and some people see things differently now, doesn't change that fact.

What shot would you remove? What scene? To make amends. To make it more palatable. To apologize. And if I did that, would you still be studying them?

Politics come and go. Politicians come and go. Only art remains.

I'm an artist. You can't make me into something I'm not.

> *She suddenly grabs the edge of the chair. She's not well. Shift. The office transforms into LENI's editing suite. LENI puts her head down on the desk, exhausted. The WOMAN transforms into KARI. She sets a cup of coffee down quietly on the desk in front of her. 1936.*

LENI (*covering her fatigue*) What's this?

KARI Dr. Goebbels sent this. He thought you might need a break.

And the post.

> *She hands LENI a pile of mail. LENI barely looks at it. Throws it down on the desk.*

KARI ...Are you all right Miss Riefenstahl—?

LENI —Yes, of course.

> *Pause.*

(*sensing her hovering*) What?

KARI The answer print for "Olympia" is back.

LENI Oh God.

> *Pause.*

How does it look?

KARI No one dared crack a tin.

> *Pause.*

LENI Well bring the goddamn thing in!

KARI rushes off and returns with an editing assistant with a huge armload of 35 mm tins. Puts them on the table. They both stand expectantly, looking at LENI.

Get out!

They exit. Silence. LENI slowly opens the top tin. Light shines out of the tin illuminating her face. The film projected.

Ancient Greece. Ruins. Statues. The relics and remains of this once great and powerful society. Through the mist, against the backdrop of their broken stone homes, pupil-less eyes stare at me. Drift in and out of view through the hazy half light.

Slowly, the statues begin to move. Silent. Naked. Wondrous. Like in a dream, breath comes to them and they come to life. And in that breath, a spark. A tiny flame. I carry the torch from its home with the poor in Olympia, through the mountains, along a shore, through Delphi, the people, the streets and finally to the Stadium itself.

Berlin.

With the crack of the starter's pistol we're off. The Führer welcomes the world. The English. India. Japan. Spain. Canada. The Americans. The German athletes march in. *Heil* Hitler! The French... no salute. But Italy! *Heil* Hitler!

Like the hundreds of thousands watching, my heart catches in my throat and I leap with tiny Marjorie Gestring, diving into the glittering sapphire blue pool far below us. I hurl the discus with commanding, powerful Schroder. I wade deep in the mud side by side with noble Jesse Owens, as he brings his eyes up and looks down the track one last time, preparing to run the race of a lifetime.

Crack!

I break the water with the divers. Half above, half under, I capture both these worlds. Their excruciatingly slow fall from the tower, then the explosion underwater as they puncture its glassy face. My tears mixing with the water and the athlete's tears as they weep at the edges of the pool. Joy. Despair.

And as the sun sets and light fades, the world changes
again. In the cool blue light of night, under the floodlights,
the athlete's bodies become more abstract, more beautiful
silhouetted against the black backdrop of night. The audience too becomes hushed, afraid to break the worshipful
silence of the intimate rites they are watching so far below.

Closing Ceremonies.

The stadium waits in expectant silence. Waiting for the
service to begin. One by one, the sky is lit by powerful
white lights that shine from the circumference of the
stadium like hands reaching up to God. Reaching up, even
as the flame quiets and finally dies in Berlin. And as
I stand amongst the people looking up at the sky, at this
holy Cathedral of Light I have helped create, I understand
what Flea meant all those years ago.

And this time I savour it.

There are these fleeting moments of such exquisite
beauty…

> *She feels a presence. Looks up. HEINZ. He puts the lid
> back on the tin. We are back in the editing suite. 1936.*

LENI   Heinz?

What are you doing here?

HEINZ   I'm not here. This is a letter.

> *He fishes it out of the pile of mail still on the tray.*

You almost missed it.

Here, I'll read it to you…

> *He opens it and hands it to her. She stares at it.*

LENI   But Heinz I have to—

HEINZ   —Leni, I'm far away and lonely… you'd better listen.

LENI   Go on then.

> *She opens the letter and reads along with HEINZ. He takes
> her for a ride around the room in her rolling office chair.*

HEINZ   Dearest Sister… I always start my letters so nicely don't you think—

LENI   —Heinz—

HEINZ   —all right.

Dearest Sister, I miss you all terribly. The Rhine is not at all what I expected. Not all pretty and charming, how it seemed in books. I've seen a few castles, but everything is shuttered up and falling apart, like the rest of the world, I guess. I'm just happy for some quiet. I sketched a flower for you on the back of this… I don't know what kind it is… but they're all over the ditches of the Rhine. A little present for you Leni. It's not much, but I know how you like your presents.

But enough of all this… Momma tells me you are terribly important now, with all sorts of friends in high places. Don't listen to what jealous people might say, big sister. It must drive them crazy to see you standing next to all those important people. Next to him. All the people *they'd* like to know.

I'm glad you have these friends. If war comes, and I think it will, you're all Momma and Father have. I know *I'm* the man, I was supposed to take care of you all, but the world is upside down—

LENI   —Heinz…

HEINZ   …I've seen things…

…and you never know what might happen.

LENI   Heinz—

HEINZ   —I just have to say it, so there it is.

LENI   Heinz what's wrong? You sound afraid—

He quickly rolls her back to her desk.

HEINZ   —that's all I wrote. I better go. You have things to do.

I'm proud of you, Leni.

He kisses her on the forehead.

Auf Wiedersehen.

> *He goes to leave. Stops.*

I almost forgot…

There's another letter. It must have gotten damp in the rain.

> *He crosses back and fishes it out of the pile on her desk.*

It's stuck to the back of this brown envelope. Knowing you, it will disappear into that mountain of paper in your apartment—

LENI —what is it?

HEINZ I don't know. But it looks important.

> *He hands it to her. She peels the small white envelope off the large brown one, where just like he has described, it has gotten stuck, and turns it over.*

LENI Paris Film Festival…

> *She rips it open and reads it.*

HEINZ Well?

LENI My film… …I'm going to Paris!

> *She throws the invite and envelope up into the air. Shift. Music. HEINZ grabs her and they dance. A wild fun Lindy Hop. The stage transforms into the party, the night of the Gold Medal Grand Prix Ceremony at the Paris Film Festival, 1937. They spin energetically with the music, full of joy. The song ends just as she is twirled around for the last time, laughing. GOEBBELS watches her. She sees him. He bows. HEINZ sees him and exits.*

GOEBBELS Where have you been? I've been looking for you.

> *LENI turns but HEINZ is gone.*

LENI I was just… dancing.

GOEBBELS You look beautiful.

LENI Thank you.

GOEBBELS   Elegant even. I've gotten so used to seeing you with pencils in your hair and a necklace of film trims, I barely recognize you.

LENI   Josef.

She joins him. They look out at the audience, who have become the crowds at the party. LENI's face changes. She is suddenly aware of people looking at her. At them.

GOEBBELS   Hey, why the long face, little bird? You won the Grand Prix.

LENI   I know.

GOEBBELS   Aren't you happy?

LENI   Of course.

LENI   This was your dream.

LENI   I know.

GOEBBELS   And?

Pause.

LENI   Why are you wearing your uniform?

GOEBBELS   What?

LENI   It makes people nervous.

GOEBBELS   Leni, I don't care what these people think. Neither should you. You've done the impossible. You've succeeded in making a film that even our harshest critics can't help but admire.

LENI   Then, why do they look at us that way?

GOEBBELS   Let them stare. They should stare. You've made a masterpiece with "Olympia" no one will ever touch. Four hundred thousand metres of film stock, Leni, cut down to four hours of flawless filmmaking. Just as you envisioned it. Every frame directed and edited by you.

The music starts up again. GOEBBELS smiles. Puts out his hand.

Dance with me?

LENI stares at him for a long moment. Finally, she takes his hand.

They dance. A slow and elegant waltz. LENI notices they are alone. She watches the audience as they dance. A dawning realization.

LENI   No one else is dancing.

GOEBBELS   You better get used to this feeling Leni. Envy…. It's everywhere these days.

The Olympics were a huge success. Thanks to you, now all of Europe knows what we're capable of. We're a force to be reckoned with. Not just another small country they can brush aside. They've appeared and competed with us on our own turf. They received our medals. They have to accept us now.

The Führer is pleased, Leni.

She stares at him. He pulls her in and they spin. The song ends.

So beautiful.

He takes one last look at her.

But Magda will be suspicious if I stay out again all night.

Don't look so sad, little bird, you're a filmmaker now. A *great* filmmaker. And not just in my eyes. In the eyes of the world. No matter what people say, you've got the Gold Medal and the Grand Prix to prove it. No one can take that away.

They almost kiss. Flashbulb. GOEBBELS exits.

REPORTER 1   Miss Rife-en-stahl!

Shift. The stage is transformed to a boat. A dock. Los Angeles. November 4, 1938.

LENI   Reef-en-stahl!

REPORTER 2   Over here! Miss Riefenstahl!

REPORTER 3   Miss Riefenstahl! Is it true you're Adolf Hitler's sweetheart?

LENI No! Of course not. *(laughs)* I see him, but, he is not difficult to see.

REPORTER 1 Miss Riefenstahl… America wants to know… what do you think about these stories circulating that Hitler has burned down Jewish businesses and homes?

LENI What are you talking about?

REPORTER 3 Surely you've heard, Miss Riefenstahl. It's all over the papers.

REPORTER 1 The newsreels. Radio.

LENI Don't be ridiculous.

REPORTER 2 There are reports that he made a speech calling for all good Germans to rid the country of the Jews—

LENI —he would never do that. That's a lie—

REPORTER 1 —so you don't believe these stories.

LENI Of course not.

> *Pause.*

REPORTER 3 Are you expecting any trouble here in America, Miss Riefenstahl?

LENI I've been *invited* here. "Olympia" won Venice and Paris… I've been invited by Universal, by—

REPORTER 2 —good luck.

REPORTER 3 Yeah, good luck.

> *They all laugh.*

REPORTER 1 Welcome to L.A.

> *They exit, leaving LENI and REPORTER 1 alone on the dock. REPORTER 1 has transformed into CHARLOTTE, a young, attractive personal assistant, who bears a striking resemblance to Snow White. November 24, 1938.*

CHARLOTTE Welcome to L.A. I'm sorry Miss Riefenstahl. I'm very sorry for all this fuss and bother.

I hope you don't mind coming through the back gate. We're doing a little renovation on the front.

Please, make yourself comfortable. I'll let him know you're here…

> CHARLOTTE exits. They have arrived in a well-appointed L.A. living room. LENI picks up a small camera sitting on a desk and examines it. We see the silhouette of a man behind her. Almost Hitler-like. LENI looks up.

LENI   *Herr* Disney.

> *He shakes her hand warmly.*

DISNEY   Miss Riefenstahl. Walt.

I'm sorry for all this bother.

LENI   No… it's fine.

DISNEY   It's a little embarrassing.

But you've had a long journey and I'm a very bad host. Can I get you a drink? Good.

> *He goes to make them each a cocktail.*

Now let's not talk about all that ugliness out there. I want to talk to you about your beautiful films.

LENI   You're very kind.

DISNEY   Not at all, Miss Riefenstahl.

LENI   Leni… please.

DISNEY   All right, Leni…

> *He hands her a drink. Considers her for a moment. Confesses.*

Our films were up against each other in Venice you know…

LENI   *(embarrassed)* Oh yes…

DISNEY   I heard from my spies how your magnificent heavyweight "Olympia" crushed my little "Snow White." It was a bit of an unfair fight, I only make films for children, but contrary to whatever you might have heard, I was proud to lose to what I hear was such an outstanding achievement.

LENI   Thank you, but you must not dismiss your film. I loved it.

DISNEY   You saw it?

LENI   Yes.

DISNEY   So… what did you think?

LENI   It's full of magic.

DISNEY   Ah. The kids like that.

LENI   But, your film's so much more than that. We were mesmerized. You're a magician with composition… and the colour, especially, I was very impressed. And that's hard for me to say. I love my black and white.

DISNEY   *(laughs)* I see. Have you ever tried animation?

LENI   Oh no… I would have no idea where to even start. But I am fascinated with how it all works. How you conjure such beautiful places out of your own mind.

DISNEY   Ah, but see that's the fun of it. With animation, you can create your own little perfect world. No matter what is going on outside.

You know, if you're curious about the process, you might like to see something I'm working on. It's a short film I like to call "The Sorcerer's Apprentice." Part of this bigger film, "Fantasia." All set to music. Almost like a concert with pictures. It's kind of experimental and a bit of a mess right now, but since you're a fellow filmmaker, and know what you'd be looking at, I think I'd be willing to show it to you—

LENI   —that would be wonderful… what's it about?

DISNEY   "The Sorcerer's Apprentice"? Well, it's just a very simple version of an old fairy tale I'm afraid.

LENI   I'm sure it's much more than that…

DISNEY   Which you might actually recognize… A humble sorcerer's assistant, who in my version is also a *mouse*, gets the opportunity to try a little of the sorcerer's power when he's left in charge of his magical cave. Now, he's supposed to fill this big vat with water, but when he finds the sorcerer's hat, he decides to try a spell of his own on some brooms to do the work for him. He ends up creating an entire army of brooms, loses control of them and it all goes horribly amuck…

LENI   And he gets in lots of trouble, I'm sure.

DISNEY   Oh yes.

> *They laugh.*

LENI   …Is that Goethe?

DISNEY   Aha! I knew you'd get it.

LENI   Little do the children know, they are listening to a good German story.

> *They laugh.*

This is nice. I don't get this opportunity you know. To talk to other filmmakers. It's too bad you were unable to come to Venice. I would have enjoyed watching both our films together with you.

DISNEY   Ah, I was busy working on this new film… and… well… I'm afraid I'm not much for festivals.

LENI   I see…

DISNEY   I never quite feel like I fit in. You know what I mean?

LENI   I do.

DISNEY   …I've always been a bit of an outsider, Leni. You and me both I think. We see things differently. We see the potential. The power of film. People are afraid of that. And with war in the air… well, it's a hard time to be an artist…

LENI   I was hoping America would be different.

DISNEY   Hopefully it will be… for you.

So… will "Olympia" get distribution here do you think?

LENI   Well, that's why I'm here, really. To see what is possible. But... I don't know. People have jumped to their own conclusions as you've probably heard... fuelled by rumours started by some German exiles apparently. So people I was to meet, Mr. Cooper... the others... are suddenly withdrawing their invitations.

Pause. It's become a bit uncomfortable.

DISNEY   I see.

LENI   *(suddenly)* Would you like to see it?

DISNEY   "Olympia"? Oh, well... yes, let me know when it screens, I know you'll find a way... and I'll try—

LENI   —not when it screens. Right now.

DISNEY   ...is that possible?

LENI   Well, I just had a thought. I'm not leaving for San Francisco for a few days... I have the reels at my hotel. I could send them over and you could watch them on your own. Just return them to me when you're done.

I would love you to see the two parts together. All four hours. I'd like to hear what you think.

Pause.

DISNEY   ...Leni... I'm not sure how to say this.

I know this may be hard to believe, but to watch your films, even in house, I would have to use a projectionist and they're all... ...well... unionized. The way this city is run, I'll be... well word will get out and...

I just can't take the chance.

She's hurt. She gets up and begins to gather her things.

LENI   I've taken up enough of your time.

DISNEY   Leni...

She's already heading for the door.

Well, at least let Charlotte help you get back to your hotel. *(calling)* Charlotte!

LENI   It's not necessary. I can take a taxi cab.

DISNEY   Leni… just let her take you.

> *Pause.*

LENI   All right.

> *It's become uncomfortable between them. CHARLOTTE appears.*

DISNEY   Well good luck, Leni.

> *He shakes her hand. He exits.*

CHARLOTTE   Miss Riefenstahl?—

LENI   —I'm at the Beverly Hills—

CHARLOTTE   —Miss Riefenstahl, you might want to make arrangements at another hotel.

LENI   What do you mean?

> *CHARLOTTE hesitates. LENI realizes something's wrong.*

What's going on? Tell me!

CHARLOTTE   There's been an announcement on the radio. They're saying… …it's been confirmed. They've burnt down Jewish synagogues and businesses. People have been killed…

LENI   *(confused)* What?

> *CHARLOTTE stands there looking at LENI.*

CHARLOTTE   In Germany.

LENI   Oh God.

CHARLOTTE   Protestors are setting up at the Beverly Hills right now. There are placards…

LENI   …I have to go….

CHARLOTTE   Should I call another hotel—?

> *She crosses to the desk.*

LENI   —not a hotel! Home…

The car's here?

Shift. CHARLOTTE transforms into the WOMAN.
Present. She is looking at LENI confused.

WOMAN   Not yet.

LENI   Miss— There's no time. I have to go.

WOMAN   *(surprised)* I'm sorry?

LENI   *(looks at her, catching herself)* …I have to go now. I said, call me a taxi.

LENI is confused. She slowly takes in her surroundings.
Realizes.

WOMAN   There's no need to take a cab, you're obviously not feeling well. I can arrange for a car and driver to take you wherever you want. I just need to call Peter—

LENI   A taxi is fine.

WOMAN   It's not a problem—

LENI   —I want to go back to the hotel—

WOMAN   —all right. Where are you staying?—

LENI   —the Beverly Hills.

Pause. The WOMAN is surprised. LENI notices. The
WOMAN says nothing. She crosses to her desk. Dials.

WOMAN   Peter, can you get a car to take Ms. Riefenstahl to the Beverly Hills Hotel please? Sure… thanks.

It shouldn't be long.

Silence. She watches LENI gather up her things. Finally.

LENI   I did it to make a point I guess.

The WOMAN says nothing.

The hotel? Oh come now, I assume that is what that look was all about.

The WOMAN still says nothing.

I don't know why I bothered. These young managers they have now, they don't remember the picketers. Christ, they don't remember the War. I've always thought people would never forget… never let go of the past. But maybe I've been wrong all along. Maybe it's just the opposite. People never remember.

WOMAN   Things change. Is that so bad?

LENI   *Evolve?*

WOMAN   Exactly.

LENI   You are so very young.

Things don't always happen in a gradual fashion. *Evolve* in some kind of gentle progression.

One day when you take a nap, you'll get up and realize that somewhere in that very short time between falling asleep and waking, everything's changed. That the world you've believed in… the person you've believed in, has transformed into something else. Oh, they have the same outline. The same shape, but when you look at them now, you see for the first time what they are. What they truly are.

You can never go back to the way it was before, no matter how hard you try.

WOMAN   That almost sounds like… regret.

LENI   Regret?

There *is* no word for what I'm talking about.

GOEBBELS   Leni!

Shift. Berlin. End of August, 1939. The precipice of war. LENI's Berlin house. GOEBBELS enters, in full uniform, with two glasses of wine.

(*urgently*) Leni? —where have you been hiding?

He hands her a glass.

The Führer is here.

LENI   What?

GOEBBELS   He's inside speaking to your father right now. Congratulating him on having such a talented and loyal daughter.

LENI   But Josef—

GOEBBELS   —what? Now you're not happy with a personal visit from the Führer?

LENI   No! It's just—

GOEBBELS   —any good German would be grateful to be so singled out for praise… for the opportunity. There are many other places he could be, Leni…

LENI   Of course, but—

HITLER   —it's all right.

> *From the doorway. Where he has been watching.*

LENI   *Mein* Führer…

GOEBBELS/LENI   *(saluting) Heil* Hitler.

HITLER   I can see exactly what she's thinking.

> *He crosses to her, a teacup and saucer in one hand.*
> *A bottle of wine in the other.*

Miss Riefenstahl is modest. She doesn't feel that she deserves special treatment.

> *Tops up her glass with wine.*

Don't sell yourself short, Miss Riefenstahl; the Third Reich owes a huge debt to you.

> *Fills GOEBBELS's glass. Hands him the bottle.*

You've helped us regain our pride. Our belief. Our confidence. Take your father. I was just speaking to him. He is a good man, Miss Riefenstahl. A good German. He remembers the old days. He knows how far we've come. He's proud of what we have accomplished. Of what *you* have accomplished. As are we all.

> *HITLER gestures to a young PHOTOGRAPHER who*
> *quickly appears. LENI and GOEBBELS join him.*

So… may this be the beginning of many more good things. For you. For us. For Germany. To Germany.

ALL   To Germany.

The PHOTOGRAPHER's flashbulb goes off. Almost sounds like a bomb. They are smiling, glasses in hand. The famous photo of the three of them.

HITLER   Ah… now we will always remember.

Pause.

Josef… take some wine to *Herr* and *Frau* Riefenstahl with my best wishes. I know they are busy preparing to come out, but they're frail. It's too chilly for them out here.

Almost an order. GOEBBELS exits, leaving the two of them alone. HITLER looks at LENI.

Well.

Uncomfortable pause.

You seem nervous, Miss Riefenstahl?

LENI   No, *Mein* Führer.

HITLER   It's all right. I understand. It's surprising to have me at your house. To see me here.

LENI   No, *Mein* Führer.

HITLER   Standing before you in a suit… not a uniform?

Having a drink under your tree.

But surely, we have worked together so closely, on all these projects that we are friends now, Leni?

Pause.

LENI   Of course, *Mein* Führer.

HITLER   So… let us talk as friends.

What are you working on?

LENI   I've been working on a film called "Penthesilea," about the Queen of the Amazons who was killed by Achilles, but it is an enormous project and… complicated.

HITLER   Why?

LENI   I was hoping to shoot right away but… it will take time to pull it all together. So, I've gone back to an old idea I've been working on since before we did "Triumph of the Will," *Mein* Führer. A much smaller film, with dance. More in the style of "The Blue Light." A small drama called "Tiefland."

HITLER   The world's on the brink of war and you're still determined to make your films. You are nothing if not persistent, Leni Riefenstahl.

> *He laughs.*

LENI   Yes, *Mein* Führer.

HITLER   So, you are only writing now.

LENI   *(confused)* Yes.

HITLER   Not shooting.

LENI   No. I have a lot of work to do on both projects, before I could possibly—

HITLER   —good. So you have some time.

LENI   Time?

HITLER   I have an assignment for you.

> *LENI is surprised.*

I want you to capture some footage of our troops. On the border of Poland. I'm not pleased with how it has been covered.

What can I say? I need your artistic eye, Leni. Your vision. To help the people really understand what is going on. These newsreels we're making right now aren't capturing it. It needs to be more powerful. Mythical.

LENI   But I know nothing about that kind of work, *Mein* Führer.

HITLER   Oh, come now, a film is a film right? How hard can it be? You make documentaries don't you?

LENI   Well yes, of course, *Mein* Führer but—

HITLER   —good. You start next week. I know you have the eye for it. Look what you've done with a rally. I want to see what you can do with a war.

> *We hear the high pitched whine of a mortar falling. LENI watches its trajectory from the audience back towards the house and HITLER. HITLER takes one long sip of tea, and as the bomb hits…*
>
> *Shift. War. Death all around. Amidst it all, LENI and a cameraman attempt to film some footage. The WOMAN appears with a clipboard. GOEBBELS pushes her down centre stage and a shot rings out. He has executed her. Then another shot. Then another. Then 28 more. LENI stands frozen, horrified at what she sees. The WOMAN killed over and over. A massacre. Konskie, Poland. 1939. A flashbulb goes off.*
>
> *Shift. The space transforms into the de-nazification court. The gunshots transform into a gavel banging. Berlin. 1952. FLEA becomes the JUDGE. The WOMAN stands up and becomes the PROSECUTOR.*

JUDGE   Quiet! Quiet please! Please continue.

PROSECUTOR   The allegations raised two days ago, relate to the events of September 12, 1939, where in Konskie, Poland, a massacre of 31 Polish Jews took place in a market square. The accused, Miss Riefenstahl, is alleged to have been present and witnessed the killings. *Revue* magazine has submitted a photo of Miss Riefenstahl, taken during the massacre, standing in the midst of other soldiers, all of whom appear to be witnessing an atrocity. They have also provided a witness who confirms that Miss Riefenstahl was there and witnessed their deaths.

JUDGE   Did she report this massacre to anyone?

PROSECUTOR   No—

LENI   —*Revue* has completely distorted the truth surrounding this photo. This disgusting tabloid has dedicated itself to

publishing groundless accusations about me since the end
of the War—

JUDGE   —Miss Riefenstahl. Please refrain from comment on
the allegations themselves. Why don't you tell us what
happened instead, in your own words.

Pause. Everyone looks at her.

LENI   I had been in the square a few days before and I saw
a group of Poles being forced to dig graves for some
German soldiers who had been killed and maimed horribly.
These Poles were being made to dig with their bare hands,
by the officers in charge. I was horrified. I spoke out. The
men turned on me and threatened me. One aimed his rifle
at me. That was the moment I was photographed.

JUDGE   So you did not see this massacre?

LENI   No. I ran away. I went to General von Reichenau to
discuss the matter of the gravediggers, and that is when
he informed me of the… incident.

The next day I resigned my post as a war correspondent
and returned to Berlin, where I have attempted, until
today, to forget these horrendous events—

JUDGE   —thank you—

LENI   —I would like to point out, that I have been tried and
cleared twice already by this court—

JUDGE   —thank you, Miss Riefenstahl—

LENI   —the past is the past. I'm innocent. Why can't you accept
that? Why can't you let it go?

The PROSECUTOR stares at her. Opens a file. Reads.

PROSECUTOR   A Telegram. Dated 1940.

From: Leni Riefenstahl

To: Adolf Hitler

"With indescribable joy, deeply moved and filled with
warmest thanks, we experience with you, my Führer, your

and Germany's greatest victory, the entry of German troops into Paris.

HITLER appears. Reading the telegram.

HITLER   You accomplish deeds beyond the powers of human imagination, deeds without equal in the history of humanity. How are we to thank you? To merely congratulate you is not enough to show you the feelings that move me."

LENI   Your,

Leni Riefenstahl.

HITLER disappears. The JUDGE hammers his gavel. The hammering transforms into a hard and punchy piece of flamenco.

Shift. LENI begins to dance. The flamenco. It builds to a crescendo—

Cut!

LENI is on the set of "Tiefland." Dancing the main scene as the character Martha. Austria, 1940. She looks tired and haggard. She's been reduced back to a tiny crew. Germany is at war.

Shit. We're going again!

The PROSECUTOR transforms into a young female PRODUCTION ASSISTANT.

ASSISTANT   Miss Riefenstahl?

LENI   What? Can't you see we're shooting?

ASSISTANT   But… we found the extras you requested.

LENI   What do they look like? Do they look Spanish? How many times do I have to explain to you people, these scenes take place in Spain, they must look Spanish.

ASSISTANT   They're Gypsies.

LENI   Good.

Well? Where are they?

The ASSISTANT holds out her clipboard for her signature on a document.

ASSISTANT   Well that's the thing. They're… they're in a kind of a camp. Near Salzburg. We need formal permission from—

LENI   —well? What the hell are you waiting for? Do I need to hold your hand?

Exasperated, LENI signs it. Shoves it back at her.

Do what you have to. We need them by next week. We need to shoot before we lose the studio again.

The ASSISTANT leaves quickly. Her crew is standing, waiting.

What the hell are you waiting for? I told you we're going again.

They quickly prepare to shoot again.

Action!

Snap back to the same hard flamenco dance. She dances as the Spanish and fiery Martha, as the war visually and aurally rages around her. The JUDGE and PROSECUTOR appear. Shift. Civil trial against Revue *magazine. 1949. Pandemonium in the court. LENI stops. She is back in court.*

PROSECUTOR   *(trying to be heard over the crowd)* Revue magazine is alleging that for her film "Tiefland," director Leni Riefenstahl explicitly requested film extras that were "Mediterranean" in appearance.

There is a quiet murmur in the court.

They are alleging that to achieve this goal, the film extras that were procured for her were Gypsies from an internment camp near Salzburg, and that Miss Riefenstahl personally selected them herself—

The noise of the court builds.

LENI   —I did no such thing—

JUDGE   —quiet please—

PROSECUTOR   —*Revue* magazine is alleging that when she was done with these extras, for her dramatic *dance* film, they were shipped off to Nazi death camps where they were killed along with mill—

> *An uproar. It's a circus.*

LENI   —that is absolutely untrue! *Revue* magazine has continued to sell thousands of magazines based on outright lies like this... complete slander! Where is the proof that any of this... any of this ever happened—?

JUDGE   —Miss Riefenstahl—

LENI   —where is the evidence—?

JUDGE   —Miss Riefenstahl—

LENI   —where are the witnesses—?

JUDGE   —Miss Riefenstahl—

LENI   —I want people to know the truth—!

JUDGE   —Miss Riefenstahl! So do we all. That's why we're here.

> *Shift. Flamenco. LENI snaps out towards us and dances as Martha one last time, building to a crescendo. She reaches out in a final gesture of longing.*

HITLER   Welcome to the Berghof.

> *Shift. HITLER's private mountain villa. The Berghof. March 21, 1944.*
>
> *He joins her. All we can hear is the wind. Side by side they both look out at the mountains. The view.*

(*quietly*) Beautiful isn't it? Obersalzberg. What a view. You can see for miles. It feels like you can see across the country. Across our new Germany.

Where have you been, Leni?

LENI   Well I was shooting in the Pyrenees in Spain, *Mein* Führer, but with everything going on, we had to move production back here to Austria.

HITLER   I see, I see… even now… always a mountain girl.

LENI   This is for that film I told you about before. "Tiefland." But the fighting's been getting very close and—

HITLER   —Why are you here?

> *Pause. She's caught off guard.*

LENI   …You called for me, *Mein* Führer.

HITLER   I did?

LENI   …yes…

HITLER   Oh yes… of course.

> *He looks at her.*

Are you hungry?

LENI   I…

HITLER   Come now. You must stay for dinner. Eva has a proper German feast prepared. She's been pining for some company. Any news from home. From the city. She hates it here, out in the mountains.

Not like you.

> *She says nothing. She looks at him.*

It's strange. Seeing you standing here in front of me, it brings it all back. Your film. That one about the young girl. What was it called?

LENI   "The Blue Light."

HITLER   Yes. "The Blue Light." The young girl who finds the crystals in the beautiful cave.

LENI   Yes.

HITLER   She finds the crystals, but the man who loves her, betrays her… am I right?

LENI   Yes.

HITLER   And the townspeople turn on her. They take her crystals and leave her nothing.

LENI   Yes.

HITLER   And when she finds the cave empty, she's broken.

And so she does the only thing left to her. She leaps off the cliff into the abyss.

Silence. He stares at the mountain.

Why are you really here?

LENI   I'm sorry?

HITLER   What do you want from me?

LENI   *Mein* Führer... you called me—

He snaps into a rage, his hand shaking. His leg shaking. His head shaking. Bluish-purple with rage, he can barely get the words out.

HITLER   —what do you want? Money? Favours? Everybody wants something! Everyone has deceived me! No one has told me the truth! The Armed Forces have lied to me! Goering! Himmler! You, you disloyal bitch! All of you, go to hell!

He shrieks at her. Into the darkness. Disappears. A gavel banging. Shift. We are back in the de-nazification trials. 1949. The JUDGE and PROSECUTOR reappear.

JUDGE   Quiet! Quiet! Miss Riefenstahl you are here today to answer the charges brought against you by Luis Trenker. Diaries, which he has produced, of one Miss Eva Braun, name you as a close "intimate" friend of Adolf Hitler's and a member of the Nazi Party. How do you answer these charges?

LENI   Luis Trenker is a liar, he's making all of this rubbish up—

JUDGE   —Miss Riefenstahl. Please answer the charges—

LENI   —how can I? They're preposterous—

JUDGE   —Miss Riefenstahl—

LENI   —he's an actor for God's sake—

JUDGE   *(to the PROSECUTOR)* Go on—

LENI   —and not even a very good one—

PROSECUTOR   —In regards to the first charge, Miss Riefenstahl, have you or have you not ever spent time with Adolf Hitler at your home? At Hitler's home… the Berghof?

> *Pause. LENI doesn't know what to say.*

(smiles) No matter. *Revue* magazine has provided me these photographs, which I will now show the court, of Miss Riefenstahl at her parent's home with Adolf Hitler and Josef Goebbels. At her own home in Berlin with Adolf Hitler and Josef Goebbels. At the Berghof with Adolf Hitler. With Josef Goebbels, Josef Goebbels, Josef Goebbels…

> *The PROSECUTOR pulls out a sheaf of photos. She could continue. Shift. The stage transforms again, leaving a lone man standing before her. GOEBBELS. 1944.*

LENI   Josef? Thank God! I've been looking for you…

> *Pause. He just looks at her.*

GOEBBELS   I've come to say goodbye.

LENI   What do you mean?

GOEBBELS   The war is here, Leni. Every man must be on the ground ready to fight by Christmas and it's my job to see that it is done.

LENI   But—

GOEBBELS   —I'm going underground.

LENI   You're leaving?

GOEBBELS   This isn't a retreat. But the Führer must be kept safe. The Russians are coming fast. Everyone has been evacuated from The *Reichfilmkammer*—

LENI   —that's what I need to talk to you about. I've been sending letters to you. To Bormann.

GOEBBELS stares at her.

Moving locations has been a disaster… I need more money. My film—

GOEBBELS   *(disbelieving)* —your film, Leni? Are you living in a fantasy world?

Berlin is under massive attack. The Russians are coming and God knows what he'll—

LENI   —but my film—

GOEBBELS   —look around you! No one cares about your god-damn film. Take your parents, whatever food and water you can carry and get the hell out of Berlin—

LENI   —But Josef—

GOEBBELS   —do it! That's all I can say. I would help you, but I can only take my wife and children. No one else.

LENI   Please—

GOEBBELS   —I can't help you anymore!

He shoves her away. She stares at him. Shift. Back to the court. De-nazification trial. 1949. The PROSECUTOR is standing holding a sheaf of photographs expectantly waiting for her answer.

PROSECUTOR   Miss Riefenstahl, please answer the question.

LENI   *(to GOEBBELS)* There was never an "intimate" relationship between Josef Goebbels and myself. Or Adolf Hitler.

GOEBBELS exits. She turns back to the PROSECUTOR, who opens her file and pulls out a piece of paper. She reads a telegram.

PROSECUTOR   A Telegram. Sent August 24, 1938.

To: Adolf Hitler

From: Leni Riefenstahl

"A congratulation given to me by my Führer is fulfillment possible: this is why my heart has moved me to give thanks.

> *HITLER appears. Reads the rest.*

HITLER   Today I embrace the roses, which are as red as surrounding mountains caressed by the last of the sun. Thus I look to the rose garden, to its gleaming towers and walls, and stroke the red flowers with my hands and know only that I am inexpressibly happy."

LENI   Your,

Leni Riefenstahl.

PROSECUTOR   Red roses on your birthday from Adolf Hitler?

> *GOEBBELS appears. Does a smart salute to HITLER who acknowledges it. They both turn and look at her.*

GOEBBELS   *Auf Wiedersehen,* Leni.

> *He suddenly and shockingly, shoots himself in the head. HITLER pulls out a gun.*

HITLER   *Auf Wiedersehen.*

> *He shoots himself. They both fall. The War is over. In disbelief, all she can do is stand and stare at HITLER's body where it fell. Shift. The court disappears. The body moves.*

FATHER   Leni?

> *Is this a dream? He slowly rolls over. Removes his moustache and jacket.*

LENI   *(terrified) Mein* Führer?

> *He puts on another coat and glasses.*

FATHER   Leni?

LENI   Father?

> *It is her father.*

FATHER   Stop sleepwalking Leni, and come and help me.

> *Shift. Night. Cold. The rubble of Berlin. He gets his suitcase, packs HITLER's things, the gun, into it. He's old. Deluded.*

LENI   It's freezing… and the middle of the night.

FATHER   Do you love your old father?

It is his old routine. His favourite.

LENI   Of course, Father.

FATHER   You must be a good girl while I'm gone.

LENI   Yes, Father.

FATHER   And you must mind your mother. Listen to her and be obedient.

LENI   *(becoming exasperated)* Yes, Father.

FATHER   And you must do your work.

LENI   Yes, Father.

FATHER   No more mooning about dancing when you should be at your work.

LENI   Father— for God's sake, I don't dance anymore—

FATHER   —Leni, I don't want to hear any more about these silly things.

And you must listen to your brother.

LENI tries to make him listen.

LENI   Father! Heinz isn't here I've told you—

FATHER   —he's the man of the house, while I'm away!

It's no use.

And do your chores.

LENI   Yes, Father.

FATHER   And not be scared at night if you hear sounds.

LENI   Yes, Father.

FATHER   And you must hug your old father.

LENI   Yes, Father.

She throws her arms around him.

FATHER   And tell him how much you love him.

LENI   *Ya,* Father.

FATHER   And promise not to miss him too much.

He'll be back one day soon.

He disengages from her and picks up his suitcase. He takes one long last look at her.

Goodbye Leni. *Auf Wiedersehen.*

He turns to go.

LENI   Father. Are you proud of me?

FATHER stops. He is confused. This is not part of his routine.

FATHER   Eh?

LENI   Of Leni.

FATHER   She's a good girl. My sweetest child.

He begins to look for her.

Where's Leni?

LENI   *(frustrated)* No, I'm right here Father. I'm Leni.

FATHER   *(calling)* Leni? She likes to hide…

LENI   She's not hiding.

FATHER   *(calling)* Leni?

LENI   She's here in Berlin, Father.

FATHER   Leni—?

LENI   —in a pile of rubble, on a street of rubble…

It's no use. He doesn't understand. He stands lost.

FATHER   You have to stop this, Leni. One day you'll run and hide and no one will come looking. Only your silly brother.

He'll find you, he'll find you, wherever you are…

He leaves. She watches him go. Shift. The present. The office.

LENI   (*still watching him leave*) I should never have come back here.

I guess I just had hope.

WOMAN   For what?

Finally the truth.

LENI   To make one last film.

Pause. The WOMAN crosses to the table, picks up the bottle of water and takes it to LENI. Holds it out. A long moment. LENI takes it. Drinks.

WOMAN   (*gently*) It just may not be the one you started out to make.

LENI looks at her.

I'm sorry if this sounds crass, I mean, I know how much you want to make "Penthesilea" but...

Have you ever thought of selling your life story?

LENI   No.

WOMAN   Why not?

LENI   It's not for sale.

WOMAN   Every A-list actress in Hollywood would kill to play Leni Riefenstahl.

Whether you wanted to or not, you've created the rarest thing in Hollywood today.

LENI   And what is that?

WOMAN   A *tour-de-force* role for an older woman.

The part of you.

LENI   It's not for sale.

WOMAN   Why not?

LENI   Because it's still mine.

Pause.

Besides... we still don't know how it's going to end.

Some people would call that dramatic tension.

A long moment. LENI looks at the WOMAN.

WOMAN   You were only partially right about me.

Beat.

I didn't decide to meet you today out of some kind of feminist guilt as you suggested earlier.

I *wanted* to meet you. I wanted to see you in person.

LENI   Why?

LENI looks at her. A long pause.

WOMAN   *(admits)* To see if I could see something that others couldn't.

Pause.

…It's what you said before. Some of it was true. I feel connected to you.

LENI   Ah.

WOMAN   But I didn't just write a paper on you.

I wrote a thesis.

LENI   I see.

Pause.

Why me?

WOMAN   I wanted to write about a woman filmmaker. And I went looking for women to write about. And there weren't any.

And then I found you. And your work was… well, it was in another class. But…

LENI   But what?

WOMAN   I felt conflicted. Because of the kind of work you did.

She says nothing.

But in the end, I did it. I chose you. I thought it would raise questions. Ask hard questions about morality. About art.

LENI   And did it?

WOMAN   I don't know.

It was like I invoked a spirit into the room that I shouldn't have. I felt it immediately.

Ambivalence.

From people in the film department. Towards you. And then, suddenly, towards me. I felt it. For picking you.

And I was suddenly confronted with this new and more disturbing question. What *does* it say? What does it say about *me*, for choosing you?

And then Aviva, my beloved professor Aviva, looked at me, and there was almost this veil, this invisible wall that came across her eyes and she said: "Why would you write about her"? And I suddenly realized she's Jewish. Of course she's Jewish, of course, but… I had never thought about it. It's not something I thought about my professors on a daily basis. Of course…. She had a perfect right to not want to work with me on this… of course…

But the thing that surprised me the most was what you talked about earlier. That easy friendship that I cherished as a student, one day it was gone and there was this unspoken divide and somehow things were changed. In the blink of an eye. They never went back to the way they were.

I had somehow unknowingly wounded her by invoking your name. By professing my fascination with you. I could see it in her eyes.

Another one, sucked in by the beauty and power of fascism.

> *Beat.*

And I had to admit. I was fascinated by you. I did find your films beautiful. I did want to meet you.

A long moment.

LENI   You said you wanted to see if you could see something that others couldn't.

WOMAN   Yes.

LENI   Well?

A moment.

WOMAN   Honestly?

Pause.

I see an old woman.

I see an old woman. Who danced one perfect dance. A dance with the devil and got what she wanted.

You stood toe to toe with some of the most powerful men in the world, not like a wife, or a secretary or a mistress… but like you belonged there. And maybe you're right; people want to punish you for that.

You have paid a high price, Leni. Your career is gone. When many others aren't. History hasn't been even-handed that way, or fair.

But you haven't paid the ultimate price.

And in the end, don't some of those people who paid for your one beautiful dance, have the right to look at me the way Aviva did? Don't they have the right to look at you?

Pause. The shadow of a figure appears in the background. PETER.

That would be your car.

LENI says nothing. She picks up her purse and coat and prepares to leave. She stops next to the desk and surprisingly holds out her hand. They shake hands.

(quietly) I hope you find what you're looking for.

Shift. The WOMAN disappears. The office disappears. The figure we thought was PETER transforms.

LENI   Heinz…

HEINZ   Hello, Leni.

LENI   Why are you here?

HEINZ   Let me tell you.

>   *He sits her down next to him.*

It was a beautiful blue day in May. I was in Russia. You've never been there, but you would love it. I know you've avoided it now for so many years, but you should go. Just once before you die. You would want to film a movie there, I know you, Leni. You would see the dramatic possibilities immediately.

You would envision a story set high in the mountains. The Ural Mountains. And the local people there would love you, of course. They would crowd around you and you would let them take turns looking in your eyepiece. I know you. You'd appreciate them and be kind to them and you'd charm them all. And you would write a splendid story. And everyone would be in it. And all the local peasants would be extras. They would play soldiers. Some to play Germans and Russians, and others to play Americans and the British of course. And Flea would shoot. And it would all build up to the final scene. And you would light it so beautifully that everyone would cry. Not just you and Momma and Father.

I wouldn't just be lying in some ordinary muddy ditch, all bloody and broken, like the others. You would place me leaning up against a tree. A beautiful tree. So I would be different. So I would stand out. Be special. Leaning back like it was the finest day in May. Arms out. Taking in the sun. And you would script it so my eyes were open, not shut. And looking up at the blue sky, not the mud. So that was the last thing I saw. Sky, not my dead comrades. My dead friends. And you would shoot me against the clouds. To show me seeing God. To make sure it was powerful and moving. Not common and inconsequential. So that people would never forget.

>   *LENI weeps. The crying of someone who has held back for decades.*

LENI   I would do that for you.

HEINZ   I know.

Goodbye, Leni.

Auf Wiedersehen.

> *He's gone. Shift. She slowly turns out to us. An echo of the opening image. Alone again.*

LENI   I can close my eyes anywhere, and in an instant, I can see it play out in front of me.

Play out in front of me like a film. Frame by frame, I can see the world emerge from the ice like a jewel from the depths of the earth. And I am that girl again.

Not some melodramatic stranded newlywed, not somebody's mistress, not filmmaker for the Third Reich... but that poor barefoot mountain girl in a story I made once when *I* was a girl.

I can close my eyes now, right here, and as if in a dream, like a ghostly somnambulist, I can feel myself rise from my bed and make my way through the silent, dark and sleeping streets to a meadow of ice, and the mountain beckons and shows me his glistening glass path and I begin to climb. My bare feet move swiftly and silently through the growing crystals of snow and ice. My body is lithe again, and I move like a silent, relentless animal to the peak and its secret that calls to me. A hollow, an unseen grotto buried deep in the mountain. My beloved crystals.

They catch the moonlight and illuminate the darkness like a sea of stars, like a sea of tiny spotlights, and for a moment in that cold blue light, you can see me, how I used to be. Before all this. Young. Beautiful. Purposeful.

> *Shift. Hard. Unapologetic.*

And I will script it so my eyes are open, not shut. And I will script it so I will be looking up at the blue sky, not the mud.

And you will prop me up against a camera, not a tree.
And you will shoot me against the clouds, to make it clear.
To show me facing God. To make sure I have my reckoning. To make sure it will be powerful and moving.

Not inconsequential and unrepentant.

And you will make it a lesson.

So people will never forget.

> *The sound of a film reel running out. Nothing more. Nothing less.*
>
> *Blackout.*
>
> *The End.*

The Red Priest

(Eight Ways To Say Goodbye)

for Ron and Ashley
partners

The Contest Between Harmony And Invention
—D. Antonio Vivaldi

In 1725, ten days before Christmas, Antonio Vivaldi published *"Il Cimento dell'armonia e dell'inventione"* a collection of four large pieces, including what we now know as "The Four Seasons." For me, his title captures the heart of the artistic process we all struggle through. The contest between harmony and invention. Between the practical and the ephemeral. Between the script and the live performance.

While we may write alone, theatre is made by many people. First of all: thanks to my parents, family and friends for their love and sustenance during this long process. Thanks to all the development partners who supported the play at various stages along the way: Ken Cameron and APN, John Murrell and The Banff playRites Colony, Jonathan Christensen & Joey Tremblay and Catalyst Theatre and Lise Ann Johnson and the National Arts Centre's On The Verge Festival. Thanks to the long list of artists who worked on various readings, workshops and first productions along the way: Michelle Chan, Charlie Tomlinson, Daniela Vlaskalic, Ashley Wright, Marian Brant, Kevin Corey, Scott Peters, Shauna Murphy, Jeff Page, Rhonda Kambeitz, Stephen Hair, Ian Leung, Glen MacGillvray, Peter Froehlich, Dave Clarke, Jen Darbellay, Karen Fleury, Dianne Goodman, Deb Howard, Darcy McGeehee, Terry Middleton, Lisa O'Brien, Scott Reid, Narda McCarroll and Cheryl Millikin. Special thanks to Bob White and Vanessa Porteous at Alberta Theatre Projects for their belief and encouragement, and the passion that the whole ATP family brought to the premiere of the play. Special thanks to Ron Jenkins and Shona Neil at Workshop West Theatre for their initial development of the play, their ongoing support and second production and for giving me a home as a writer.

But most of all to Ron and Ashley, who have been my partners since the very beginning.

Beginning to write has been an amazing and rewarding journey. And a journey as intangible as the contest Vivaldi describes. As intangible as redemption. As hope. As a garden. As a concerto. As a fellow believer.

I hope you enjoy the play.

—Mieko Ouchi, 2003

The Red Priest (Eight Ways To Say Goodbye) premiered at Alberta Theatre Projects in Calgary, Alberta, Canada as part of the National playRites Festival of New Canadian Plays, February 8, 2003 with the following company:

WOMAN	Mieko Ouchi
VIVALDI	Ashley Wright

Director	Ron Jenkins
Set Designer	Scott Reid
Costume Designer	Jenifer Darbellay
Lighting Designer	Terry Middleton
Composer	Dave Clarke
Choreographer	Darcy McGeehee
Production Dramaturg	Vanessa Porteous
Production Stage Manager	Dianne Goodman
Stage Manager	Deb Howard
Assistant Stage Manager	Karen Fleury
University of Calgary Intern	Lisa O'Brien

The playwright gratefully acknowledges the development assistance of:

Alberta Playwrights Network
Alberta Theatre Projects National playRites Festival of New Canadian Plays
The Banff playRites Colony—a partnership between the Canada Council for the Arts, The Banff Centre and Alberta Theatre Projects
The National Arts Centre (English Theatre), and the On The Verge Festival
Workshop West Theatre

Setting

The Majority of the action takes place in Paris, the month of May, 1740.

❧ MOVEMENT ONE ❧

Part One: Presto

Blackout.

A WOMAN dressed in the 18th century trappings of the rich French noblesse, and a MAN dressed in a richly embroidered coat and breeches, all in black, enter the stage and freeze in silhouette.

Vivaldi's Summer Presto from "The Four Seasons: Concerto in G minor."

Sting one of music: the WOMAN poses dramatically.

Sting two: snaps her fan open. Fans.

As the main body of the piece begins, the WOMAN leaves her pose and strides through her garden speaking loudly to an unseen and trailing gardener.

WOMAN   Monsieur Vallée, by tomorrow morning at 8 o'clock sharp, I would like all the flowers in the beds of the West Parterre to be replaced by flowers in "white." I will be holding a walking party in the late morning, and I would hate for my guests to be disturbed by any colour that might be too harsh for such an hour. By four o'clock however, they may be changed back to their original blue and yellow arrangement.

Garish I know, but my husband likes it that way.

Blackout on the WOMAN. Music out.

The Presto begins again. Lights up on the MAN. He bows on an imaginary violin with a real bow. Violin solo in the Presto. It is VIVALDI.

VIVALDI   What are you staring at?

He turns his back on the audience. He turns back with the music.

What? Waiting for a word of wisdom from the touched?

This is how it happened. I awoke one morning at my *conservatorio*, at the *Ospedale Della Pieta*, where for years I had taught my darling girls how to sing and play in tune, and realized that people were recognizing me in the street and that somehow, like in a dream I had slept through, I had become the desired dinner guest, the passionate Red Priest that all the women pined for. And how? By playing my violin. As I had always done.

Violin solo.

Music is something people have always loved to admire. The ability to write and play the invisible structure that others can't see... that is what they crave, to see someone do and create something they know they can't... that is completely and impossibly beyond their reach.

And you, like them, will pay for it.

Blackout.

Part Two: The Walking Party

Vivaldi's Andante from the "Concerto for Two Mandolins in G Major." The WOMAN is instantly quiet, reposed, fluid and charming. A mask. The audience is now her late morning walking party.

WOMAN   Friends... my husband says that today's most ideal form of garden, *Le Jardin de la Raison*, is in his mind, embodied by the perfect Royal Garden at Versailles: *Le Parterre du Midi*. In this most faultless composition, a simple rectangular garden is focused on a central fountain, located at the crossroads of four gravelled walks. Years ago, water here used to be a well. Now, its fountain functions simply as a... well... beautiful and decorative accessory...

Or as another example of man's triumph over the slippery bits.

These days... they say... men go to great lengths to bring water over vast distances to feed thirsty gardens across France. They say, that the fourteen hundred fountains at Versailles are so demanding that nearby rivers have been dammed and terraced in a desperate attempt to create the water pressure they require but... to no avail... and... *(She looks around and whispers conspiratorially.)* ...that several famous and talented gardeners such as Le Vau and Le Nôtre, have gone *mad* in the trying.

> *She sees the tree temple and steps through it gracefully.*

Ah.... One of my husband's recent and most astounding propositions for this garden are the *palissades*. Trees which, when twisted and trained into classical columns, form a temple.

(to her trailing friends) Beautiful in execution don't you think?

> *She steps through and walks along a path to the corner of the garden.*

Ah... the peace and quiet of the geometric paths. Nothing out of order.

> *A hint of a smile.*

Well... they say.

> *Blackout.*

Part Three: Taming the Horses

> *VIVALDI is drunk and in a room with an unseen prostitute. Vivaldi's "Concerto for Two Violoncellos in G Minor."*

VIVALDI   When I play for you my darling... and play so well... do you wonder, along with everyone else in France and Italy, with your simple and slack-jawed awe, if my inexplicable dexterity comes from the very Devil himself? Skills created through a musical pact that you mere mortals are not aware of?

Silence. Not surprising. Didn't pay you for your conversation.

They say, a courtier saw the Devil standing right next to me one night as I played, even conducting the bow and fingers at times. When questioned, the courtier swore that this Devil was red in colour, had small but vicious horns and a long forkèd tail, snaking out between his feet. Well, well, well... how could you possibly argue with such an accurate and detailed vision? And who cares about the rumours anyway? Doesn't it bring on the crowds? What do you imagine I wonder?

There is a silence in the music. He considers her.

(*a hint of cruelty*) Hmmm... what do you think... what do you think? Ah! That I learned this inimitable skill by practicing my scales pathetically day in day out, year in year out in a windowless cell, chained to my chair by a kindly idiot, an unintentionally cruel and brutal father that didn't understand that children need sun and air to grow?

Or... do you imagine that as a young man, I felt a love: passionate, gut-wrenching... illicit, for a wealthy, married woman only to be discovered by her jealous and humiliated husband? Never to see her again? And that this pushed me spirit-broken to the violin, this seemingly human and compassionate instrument?

Or... that a lonely life as an *Abbé*, a holy priest, sentenced to years teaching musical scales to young orphan girls, ripe, luscious and damaged as they often are, gave way to guilty nights alone with the violin in my room... empty... unfulfilled... abandoned?

He takes a drink.

Or my darling... far more crassly and cruelly, do you imagine that this life, full of whores like you and drink, keeps me chained to this instrument simply as a way to pay for it all? Which is it, eh?

He takes another drink. Silence. Cello solo. He looks at her.

An angel?

...an explanation I would have never considered.

Blackout.

Parts Four and Five: A Minuet

The WOMAN stands in the corner of the central square of the garden. She curtsies.

WOMAN   Eight ways to say goodbye:

A minuet by J.S. Bach begins. "Orchestral Suite No. 2 in B Minor." She begins to practice a minuet.

(as she steps along one side of the square—sweetly) One and Two and Three and Four and Five and Six and Seven and… Eight.

VIVALDI counts along with her on this first set of eight, as he conducts a group of unseen students. In English.

The WOMAN turns smartly in the corner to face the next side of the square. Second set of eight. In perfect time.

I hate you. *I* love another. *I'm* bored. *I'm* tired. *I'm* young. *I'm* lazy. *I'm* sly. And I'm reconsidering.

She turns again smartly in the corner to face the next side. Third set of eight.

Un et Deux et Trois et Quatre et Cinq et Six et Sept et…. Huit.

VIVALDI counts along with her again, as he continues to conduct his students for this third set of eight. This time in Italian. They are not doing very well.

She turns to the final corner. Fourth set of eight.

You hate me. *You* love another. *You're* bored. *You're* tired. *You're* old. *You're* busy. *You're* cowardly. And you're reconsidering.

She curtsies. Blackout.

✦ MOVEMENT TWO ✧

**Part One: Eight Ways to Say Goodbye—
A Breeze and Nothing More**

*The WOMAN crosses slowly to a fountain and pulls
herself up precariously onto the ledge. Vivaldi's "Concerto
for Cello in B flat." Largo. She weaves on delicate heels
around its ledge, tempting the water with her dress.*

WOMAN   Eight ways to say goodbye:

Public indiscretion causing social humiliation. Private
indiscretion causing children. Refusing access to my bed.
Laughing at my own jokes at court. Consorting with
people of low humour and wit. Appearing physically
ungainly. Not dressing well.

Supporting poor artists of an inferior quality.

If I go… he'll erase all trace of me here as if I never
existed. Just like this garden…

A garden is beautiful… yet ephemeral as a bloom because
of its very transitory nature. Two hundred years from
now, nothing will be left here but bones. The bones of a
garden. No flowers. No order. No flesh. Just a skeleton of
architectural remains and ruin.

> *She climbs off the fountain and with passion begins to walk
> among the trees in the forest pushing at them angrily with
> speed and momentum as she goes. Second phrase of the
> music.*

Eight ways to say goodbye: Goodbye. I hate you. I love
another. I don't love you anymore. You don't make me
laugh. I want to be alone. Despite the things that bind us,
there are too many unsaid things, un-discussed moments,
lies that don't add up, stories that should be forgotten,
cruelties that can't be forgotten, things you don't understand and things that I don't understand that just make
me feel that—

*She stops at the edge of the forest and calmly crosses back
through the wildly swaying trees untouched to the centre
of the forest.*

As I retrace my path back to the house, my heavy dress
erases my footsteps in the fine gravel… eliminating all
sign of me as I pass.

*She turns slowly and exits to the house through the forest.
The trees sway gently as if nothing more than a breeze had
passed through. Blackout.*

Part Two: Eight Ways to Say Goodbye—The Letter

*VIVALDI alone in the garden. Vivaldi's "Violin Concerto
in D Major." Largo. On the violin solo as it begins.*

VIVALDI   Eight ways to say goodbye:

Overly modest playing in the presence of a patron. Overly
excessive playing in the presence of other composers.
Embellishment of other's compositions, even when it is an
improvement. Producing your own operas. Lack of a lover
of rank and wealth. Lack of a family who were sufficiently
poignant and poor. Admitting a need for money in an age
of excess. And most of all… oh most of all…

…an un-dramatic and ordinary death.

He pulls out a letter.

After everything I've done. I've achieved. I've sacrificed.
To be like them. To fit in. To be respected. These people
despise me. They can sniff out money in your pores like it
was perfume. I'm still the hired help.

But if I go back… who will even know me?

Once long ago, the *Ospedale Della Pieta* was my home…
There I was someone. I was *Maestro di Concerto! Maestro!
Maestro!* They would call out my name as they ran down
the halls… all my little girls. They *loved* me.

But now… the most severely blemished, the crippled and
unsightly, are nuns. Their life is God. Others, the pretty

ones, the ones who carry their scars on the inside, they
have escaped with the boys who called to them… the
gondoliers and serving boys, who watched with love as
they passed by in the streets singing with the voices of
angels. Or with the rich men hunting for wives behind the
grills of the church lofts.

So here I stand. Death in poverty or a life in prostitution…

He looks at the letter again. He decides.

All statues are made of snow. Everything falls apart.
Everyone is forgotten.

The piece ends. In silence. The sycophant.

(dictating) "Most Highest Grace…. Thank you for your
most recent letter. If, as you have promised, Your Excellency
would be kind enough to complete my happiness, it
would be sufficient to honour me with but one precious
command, which would compensate for the pain of being
so far away from you in Italy. I pray that this command
may be that I give you proof of my profound veneration
and respect through the creation of a few poor concertos
for your enjoyment.

*Behind him, the WOMAN enters, looks at him and
continues the letter. Reading it on the other end.*

WOMAN   I thank your illustrious Grace for the benevolence
and inborn kindness you have shown on my feeble efforts
of the past, and hope that I may compose a new piece that
will please your most discerning, indulgent and generous
eye. I hope that I may look forward to another visit to the
astonishing city of Paris. And of course, to the most
exquisite home of you and your wife.

They both step forward to the audience.

BOTH   Your humble, devoted and obedient servant. Don
Antonio Vivaldi."

They turn to each other, VIVALDI passing her the letter.

Part Three: The Concert

The opening strains of "La Stravaganza: Concerto #12 for Orchestra in G Major." Largo. They bow to one another. We are instantly in Paris. We are in the home of the WOMAN and her husband. A private concert for them and their guests.

VIVALDI   Your Excellency.

VIVALDI bows.

WOMAN   That was an extraordinary performance, *Maestro.*

VIVALDI   You thought so, Your Grace? You honour me with your pleasure at my simple, unaccompanied piece. Your gracious favour makes my humble labour all the more worthwhile.

WOMAN   My husband saw you play at court some time ago and still remarks upon your astonishing ability. He told me that the privilege of witnessing you play would be one of his greatest memories.

I see now that he was not exaggerating.

The music ends at the end of the first musical phrase. VIVALDI bows again.

Thank you for playing for us tonight after such a long journey. But before our guests descend upon you… a moment?

She holds out her hand. Expectant. He quickly takes it and helps her to sit. Pause.

As you know from his letter, my husband is sincere in his offer of patronage.

VIVALDI bows again.

Please. He is a great lover of the arts as you know, and hopes his simple support of your work may bring forth many new compositions that the world may share and marvel at. Perhaps even one or two dedicated to him…

VIVALDI   Of course, Your Excellency—

VIVALDI bows again.

WOMAN   —as for the other matter he mentioned, he hopes
and expects *me* to begin at once. Will you be willing to
accommodate his somewhat… rash and silly request?

VIVALDI   Your Grace, I was unsure at first when he proposed
this… this… arrangement.

WOMAN   I realize that my abilities are far below those whom
you usually tutor.

VIVALDI   Oh no no no no no…. Your Grace that is not at all
what I meant. As you may know, I taught for many years
to young girls, and I believe that every child has the ability
to play and appreciate music…

She looks at him.

I simply meant to say that I was unused to teaching
a woman of your… well… …status and illustrious
upbringing.

WOMAN   Believe me, *Maestro*; the cost of my dress is not equal
with my ability as a violinist. If it was… I shouldn't need
you.

She considers him a moment.

Is it because I'm a woman? If you require assurances,
Maestro, I assure you, my intentions are completely
musical.

VIVALDI   Of course, Your Excellency.

WOMAN   *(letting him off the hook)* I hope it relieves you to hear
that I am simply learning the violin to please my husband.
He feels my melancholic nature may be helped by the
study of music. He also desires that I cultivate some of the
finer arts, so that I may entertain him and our guests in
our home and at court, as you have done this evening. Not
as well as you of course…

VIVALDI   *(bowing)* Your Excellency.

WOMAN   In fact, he has arranged for the most extraordinary thing, *Maestro*. He has arranged for *me* to play for the Court.

VIVALDI   Ah…

WOMAN   In six weeks.

VIVALDI is shocked. She continues.

That is the short time you'll be staying with us is it not? It is… a sort of courtly bet… as you might describe it… between friends. The King has heard of your work with the girls at the *Ospedale*… you've made quite the name for yourself there as a brilliant teacher… and His Highness and my husband have made a bet to see if you can duplicate the feat with me.

Pause.

VIVALDI   The King. I see.

Pause.

Your Excellency, if I may be so bold… the potential for humiliation is…. …What is *your* motivation for doing it?

WOMAN   For myself? Well I cannot confess to any real desire to play an instrument of any kind. But I will comply, simply as the duty of a loving wife to please her husband. Do you take issue with *that* as a motivation, *Maestro*?

VIVALDI   …of course not.

WOMAN   Very well then. I look forward to beginning our lessons.

He nods and bows deeply again. She exits. He looks after her. A mystery.

Part Four: The First Lesson

Vivaldi's "Concerto for Lute and Two Violins in D Major." Opening Allegro. An almost ugly sound. The WOMAN crosses downstage and faces out, waiting for instruction. VIVALDI brings the violin to her and places it on her shoulder. As he begins to correct her position, his back to the audience, she turns to the audience.

WOMAN   I hate him. Hard fingers force my wrist into position.
Over and over. Like I'm a child, incapable of my own
corrections. Repeat. Repeat. Repeat. Again. Again. Again.
Never-ending corrections like Father. "Loosen the grip…"
as if I mean to do it incorrectly. Tighten. Relax. Firmer.
This is endless. I'll die of boredom. I'd rather be in bed. I'd
rather be at Court. I'd rather be anywhere but here.

>   *They spin and reverse positions. VIVALDI faces out; the
>   WOMAN faces the back wall. To the audience.*

VIVALDI   When did we last eat? These wealthy people who
live in the country. They seem to be able to exist on
a crumb of baguette and some Brie and wander for hours
about the gardens talking of wig styles. Meanwhile the
honoured guests starve. No. Back to the moment at hand.
(to her) Loosen. Loosen the wrist. Not a grip but a caress.
You're not holding a pot…

>   *The WOMAN gives him a withering look and looks away.
>   He moves onto something else.*

(to himself) No. Place her head correctly on the shoulder of
the violin… *(he does—to her)* Correct. Replace. Again.
Again. *(to himself)* So she can memorize the position.
Please memorize the position. *(to her)* No. Loosen your
shoulders. Release the neck. *(He pulls her sharply. Too
sharply. She resists. A standoff.)* I pull her too sharply. Trust
me. Give in to the correction. *(She allows him to replace her
head delicately in the correct position. Now to her.)* Don't
tighten. *(She makes absolutely no change.)* Yes!…

>   *They turn and switch position again. To the audience.*

WOMAN   Why did he agree to this…? He's only doing it for
the money. I can smell his desperation seeping through the
snuff and the perfume. He knows he's on his way out of
favour and a day away from the street. Soon he'll be playing for his supper… bedding down at night with some
poxy woman… dying of starvation, drink, disease…

I dream at night of dying. No unnoticed, inconsequential
death for me of course. I dream of a delicious death. One
that will be the talk of the Court for decades to come.

Infamous. Incomprehensible. One they can't erase. Hanging from a tree in the garden. Drowned. Stabbed. Poisoned.

They turn and switch again. To the audience.

VIVALDI   Yes! Poisoned by my own hand. It's a miracle I'm still alive, *sono vivo*, considering the playing I've had to suffer through. No matter what any learnèd philosopher or drunken cardinal tells you about the violin being the glorious voice of angels come down from heaven… someone *learning* the violin is another story.

The piece of music ends.

And now…

He very dramatically reveals the bow to her, for the first time.

…The bow.

She takes it and makes a horrible bow hold. He winces.

Place it gently on the string.

She places the bow tentatively on the string.

A single stroke to test the position.

She looks at him with apprehension. Really? He nods. She plays. A horrible note. A beat. How best to comment…

No.

Pause.

Stroke the strings. Don't punish them. Don't punish me.

He laughs. She doesn't. Back to work.

Now…

Another horrible note no better than the first.

Better…

He's lying and she knows it. Another note.

Better!

She continues to play the single notes until a soft bell rings. She turns and holds the violin out to him. Beat. Explaining.

WOMAN   My husband.

He takes it. She goes to exit.

VIVALDI   Your Excellency, thank you for your most gracious and benign patience with me... you have done well, very well today—

He bows.

WOMAN   —I'm not sure that holding a violin like a pot is considered doing well...

Nevertheless.... 'Til the next lesson?

She leaves abruptly. He stares after her.

Part Five: The Sadness

VIVALDI alone in the forest. Dawn. Dark and lonely. Vivaldi's "Concerto in D Major for Cello." Adagio (Affectuoso). Caught up in the memory.

VIVALDI   I think about the days when I would get up early, trailing the chill off my shoulders like a foggy cape and striding across the *conservatorio* piazza towards my beloved music room, where I would prepare for the day, simply... so simply... build up the fire... warm the hands... ahhh the day's work. What do the girls know so far? What notes can they hit? How many sopranos do I have? How many altos? Will the younger violins be able to play the difficult passage I wrote last night, for the tribute when His Excellency, King Augustus comes to visit? Perhaps I should simplify...

...And then suddenly... inevitably... it just didn't matter anymore...

He comes out of his reverie back to the present.

Who gives a second thought about the musical future of young girls when there are kings to please...?

Blackout.

❧ MOVEMENT THREE ❧

Part One: The Opera

Another night. A masque ball after a large dinner for many guests. The opening strains of the first movement, the allegro, from the Spring section of "The Four Seasons" begin. VIVALDI looks pained. It has become a ball and chain.

VIVALDI   Ah… "…The Four Seasons."

He drinks deeply.

WOMAN   *(watching him from the back of the room)* My husband made all the arrangements that we might hear your piece in its entirety this evening. He is, as you know, a great admirer of this particular composition.

VIVALDI   Ah… of course, Your Excellency.

He bows. She puts her hand out expectantly. He goes to her. As the scene progresses, they complete a minuet together, speaking as they dance.

WOMAN   If I may ask *Maestro*, what is *your* opinion of this composition? It has made you famous. Is it, as it appears to be for so many others, your favourite composition?

VIVALDI   I… …well… I am of course most grateful for the immense affection that has been showered upon such a small and humble piece, Your Excellency, and its popularity at so many evenings such as this one.

They cross to the front of the room. An opportunity.

And which, of course, Your Excellency, wouldn't be possible without the gracious support and commissions of many patrons of the highest order, such as your husband.

They bow to her husband and others in the loge seats in the ballroom.

WOMAN   But is it your *favourite*, Maestro?

VIVALDI   I… well…

She looks at him. The dance begins.

I… I will admit it here, being in such esteemed and knowledgeable company this evening… that to be completely truthful, Your Excellency… I prefer the opera.

WOMAN   Really?

VIVALDI   Like many, Your Excellency, I am most enthralled with the dramatic spectacle, the emotion and *bravura* of the singers, and of course the excitement of Carnival that reigns in the loges of the theatre. For a humble priest like myself, an evening at the opera is, if I may say, quite… intoxicating.

WOMAN   But of course you *produce* them…

VIVALDI   Yes! Indeed I do.

> *He laughs uncomfortably, hoping for a way into his real purpose. Nothing.*

WOMAN   I have heard that you have written for some *castrati*, Maestro.

VIVALDI   *(thankful for her interest)* Ah yes, Your Excellency!

WOMAN   Here in France, there are many, including the greatest philosophers, who look down on this practice as barbaric. They believe emasculation is not worthy of a modern, enlightened society.

VIVALDI   Ah…

WOMAN   These *capons*, are they happy?

VIVALDI   *(taken aback)* Your Excellency, I believe they are. In Italy, they are showered with money and adulation, and their names are known by one and all.

WOMAN   There are many here who find their voices almost laughable.

VIVALDI   To my humble taste, Your Excellency, and to the taste of many in Italy, they are some of the most extraordinary singers of our time. Senesino, Caffarelli… the great Farinelli, I am most privileged to say, has performed in two of my operas.

WOMAN   I would have thought that working with a priest would have made him uneasy.

> *VIVALDI is not sure what to say.*

My husband says that he has heard a rumour that lately Farinelli has taken to wearing a brazen gold embroidered waistcoat that blinds the *Abbati* in the front rows of the orchestra when the lamps are brought out.

I think it serves them right for what they did to him... if you know what I mean?

> *She smiles. He is confused. She makes a scissor action with her fingers. Chop. Chop.*

VIVALDI   Of course, Your Excellency.

> *Uncomfortable pause. A chance.*

If I may... may I describe to you my latest opera, *L'Olimpiade*? It has just opened in Siena to some excellent notices, its second production, and is based on the mythological story of the gods—

WOMAN   —How fascinating—

VIVALDI   —in particular, I think you would find the part of Megacle, the tragic hero, to be most moving—

> *The piece ends.*

WOMAN   *Maestro.*

> *The WOMAN bows and heads back to her seat, leaving VIVALDI to trail after her.*

VIVALDI   In fact, I am hoping that some support from interested and knowledgeable parties may assist me in bringing the piece here to Paris, where it may be enjoyed by His Highness the King and others of great taste and esteem like His Excellency, such as... your husband.

> *The WOMAN looks at him.*

(realizing)...And *you*, of course, Your Excellency. I did not mean to infer that you did not also enjoy the opera.

> *She looks at him.*

WOMAN   Me? Oh no I never go… I hate the theatre.

> *Explains.*

The smell.

Now if you will excuse me… I hope that you enjoy listening to your most… beloved composition *une fois encore.*

> *She hands him her glass. VIVALDI bows deeply. She exits. "The Four Seasons" continues. He looks after her. He drinks.*

Part Two: A Dream

> *Music continues. Spring from "The Four Seasons." The second movement. Largo. The WOMAN enters.*

WOMAN   A dream.

I'm standing in my room. It's my wedding day. I'm standing in my corset and paniers. My arms out, I turn slowly as three young serving girls blow the finest white powder onto my body off pieces of parchment. Three young girls, no older than me. They blow and blow until I am covered from head to toe with the finest mist of powder. A ghost. They slowly turn me to face the mirror. They lift the heavy gown over my head and dress me without disturbing a particle. They place the lace veil on my head. It's time. They lead me outside. To the church. To the waiting crowds inside. To my mother and father. Father: austere and nodding. Pleased. Mother: unclear. A mixture of hope and fear together. They all look at me expectantly. I walk down the aisle. See him there. Every muscle in my body is telling me to run and yet I continue towards him. One foot after the other. My blood is in my ears. Pounding with every heartbeat. I can't breathe. I reach his side. We turn to look at one another. He's old. With stern eyes and a tight mouth. I feel my breath leaving me.

Then suddenly, somewhere, I hear the tiny bell-like sound of the tap of a baton on the edge of a music stand. And then like from heaven, a sound.

A choir of girls.

I look up but I can't see them. They're hidden behind the grills, but I can see their eyes and their mouths as they begin to sing, through the diamond shaped holes of the screens. The Cardinal is speaking. The singing gets louder and louder. Now my husband. His voice drowned out by the voices of the girls as the piece builds. He looks expectantly at me now. Sharp eyes focused on my lips. Waiting for me to speak, but the girls are like thunder now. And in an instant, I am one of them. My breath is their breath. Their eyes are my eyes. My voice is their voice.

And with the last echo of their voices as they finish, I'm gone.

Blackout.

Part Three: Another Lesson… The Orange

VIVALDI enters the garden. Vivaldi's "Concert for the Prince of Poland." Andante. He crosses to the wine. He needs a drink. He throws back one glass in one shot. Another. Pours himself a very full third glass and turns to find the WOMAN sitting silently, watching him. The terrace of the garden. He quickly puts the glass down and turns and smiles, public face on.

VIVALDI   Your Excellency—

She looks at him coldly. Impassively. No hint of what she is thinking.

WOMAN   —the least you could do, *Maestro*… is offer me a drink as well.

VIVALDI   I— *(He starts to make an excuse but changes his mind.)* …I am of course your most humble servant.

He pours her a glass of wine and takes it to her. She accepts it and he sits down. Silence.

WOMAN   That was quite an evening. You were very entertaining, *Maestro*… I thought your stories were funny, if a bit restrained.

VIVALDI You are a very gracious hostess, Your Excellency, I am most sincerely grateful for these weeks of hospitality both you and your husband have afforded me.

WOMAN But even the women appreciate a little ribaldry you know…

He nods. Silence. A painful silence. Finally.

We really have nothing to say to one another do we? Other than the usual pleasantries…. That's all right. You're not paid for your idle conversation are you? You're a violinist… a virtuoso… a composer… a great *maestro*…

…And yet, here you are…

You must admit… you've really come down in the world to spend your days with me.

VIVALDI says nothing.

Silent still. Even when provoked. And yet, why should that surprise me? That has been your demeanor around me since you arrived in our house.

But I've heard from courtiers, from past patrons that have supported you, that you cut quite the figure in certain circles… especially with a few glasses of wine in you. That you can be devastatingly cruel to those who admire you… or ask you to give them advice… or try to study your skill. That you make people cry. Quit the violin. Find other professions. So why hold back from me? Why so kind? Well, perhaps *kind* is a little overstated… *restrained* at least… I've obviously no talent…

VIVALDI Your Excellency, you have a wonderful—

WOMAN —please.

He has no response. She considers him. A chance.

What are you so afraid of? That your commission will be cut off if you offend me? I don't pay it…

VIVALDI No.

WOMAN   My husband does. Just as he buys my clothes and keeps me in this beautiful house. And I… am not my husband.

VIVALDI   No.

WOMAN   Well then… talk to me like I'm one of your students. Tell me! Why are you so gentle with me? Why go so against your natural disposition? Surely you're not that desperate for money. Your name still carries some power in Venice…

> *No answer.*

Well?

VIVALDI   Your Excellency…

> *Pause. What the hell.*

You don't care.

WOMAN   Pardon?

VIVALDI   You don't care about the violin. Oh you say you admire it… you admire my ability to play it… but you don't. And you don't want anything from me. In fact, I haven't seen any evidence that you respect me in any way.

WOMAN   Really?

> *She is taken aback.*

VIVALDI   *(bolder)* Considering your lack of interest for music, I've wondered for quite some time in fact, why you're here with me at all—

WOMAN   —I've told you.

VIVALDI   Ah yes… to learn the violin… to please your husband. To win a bet.

WOMAN   You don't believe me?

VIVALDI   Hmmm…

WOMAN   You think I'm lying?

VIVALDI   Doesn't quite ring true.

WOMAN   Oh really? So what do you propose as *your* theory? I'm looking for a lover and you're some sort of hired suitor? Aha… you *have* been waiting on pins and needles for the demand to come haven't you? The call to my bed? Even now… alone in the garden… it's made your heart race hasn't it… you're thinking… is this the moment?

VIVALDI   No.

WOMAN   Hmmm. Maybe you think I'm a studied dilettante that dabbles in the arts… one of those rich married women whom you met tonight, who pathetically trail their fingers through painting, music, drama? Student of all… mistress of none?

   Pause.

VIVALDI   A… kind of suicide.

   Pause.

WOMAN   What can you possibly mean by that?

VIVALDI   Death by court.

   I recognize it as a fellow believer. Believe me, it's crossed my mind as well.

WOMAN   You think I want to destroy myself by failing at court…

VIVALDI   Why not? You have the perfect opportunity. A ridiculously imminent and potentially degrading solo performance for the most powerful in France. All your friends and rivals. A bet that will determine your husband's future at court. If you fail… he'll have the proper excuse to begin to banish you… "She's not feeling well…" "She's visiting friends in the country…" "She's gone mad…" Any number of excuses. People will nod sympathetically. "Take a mistress." Because they'll understand his position. And you…

   …Well… you'll be free.

WOMAN   Free? Not exactly.

VIVALDI   Believe me, giving in to the inevitability of living alone and penniless has begun to seem more and more appealing. Relief. I know you've never experienced it, but you'd be surprised how wonderful a life of simplicity is.

WOMAN   It's an absurd suggestion. What possible reason would I have to run away from my husband, and all of this, to a life of… poverty? Any theories about that, *Maestro*?

VIVALDI   No…. None yet. But I'm watching.

Silence. She considers him for a long moment.

WOMAN   Since we have put our public faces aside and are being frank if not a little fantastical with one another, I think it's my turn to ask you a question, *Maestro*… you speak so sentimentally of the past… …what was your life like? Before all this?

VIVALDI   Before I was famous?

She nods.

Difficult question. Most simply I was poor. But I could play the violin. And because I showed promise, the *Abbati* took pity on me and took me in. We struck a bargain. They made me a musician. In return I became a priest.

WOMAN   The Red Priest.

VIVALDI   The Red Priest.

I'm sure you imagine the life of a priest is mysterious. It isn't. I taught young girls to play instruments and sing. And somehow we became the fashion. A curiosity. The *Abbati* were uneasy about women in church… made them play behind grills. That only added to their appeal. So… I haven't answered your question… *(searches)* What was it like? It was… easier. Full of hunger at times… worries… same as now at times, but clear. My goals were clear. My motives were clear. *Clear-er* anyway. I didn't think about things as much as I do now. I hadn't achieved anything that anyone cared about, so I didn't know what it would be to fear losing all that. And that lack of fear gave me a kind of freedom.

WOMAN   You miss that… freedom?

VIVALDI   I miss that.

>   *Pause.*

WOMAN   So why are you here then? And not back at your school?

>   *Pause. He looks at her. His turn.*

VIVALDI   Have you ever lived outside of court?

>   *No answer.*

But you think of it… you've thought of it… am I right?

>   *She stares into space.*

Suddenly I am the one to talk and you're the silent one.

>   *She stands abruptly and smiles.*

WOMAN   I was only thinking. You haven't commented on my garden, *Maestro*. What do you think? What do you think of my beautiful garden?

VIVALDI   *(looks and shrugs)* It is a… beautiful… garden.

WOMAN   Ah… but like your violin, it is so much more than that… to some of us. Oh, I know you have wondrous gardens in Italy, but really, you must admit, the world has never seen the sheer flawlessness of the conception and execution of the modern French Garden. The absolute perfection of it all. It is in so many ways the outdoor equivalent to your Italian operas… what do you think?

>   *He looks at her.*

Look again. Try to appreciate it. This garden is perfect.

VIVALDI   And this gives you pleasure?

WOMAN   Oh more than that. It's the skeleton that holds me up some days. I depend on its predictable regularity. I need its symmetrical beauty. Without that… …well I'm sure you know exactly what I speak of. We each have our skeletons no?

>   *He looks out at the garden again.*

VIVALDI   It's not at all comparable to an opera, least of all an Italian one. For all its perfection and beauty… where is the chaos? The emotion? The passion? *(beat)* The human spirit?

> *She looks at him for a long time. She walks slowly to one of the trees and picks an orange from it.*

WOMAN   Consider… an orange. Delicate, fragile, juicy… exotic. What a lot of fuss has occurred that this orange thrived long enough to be picked so luxuriously by me this night. How many people's lives have centered on the survival of this sole orange?

Seeds carried in carriages over miles and borders, wrapped in burlap, packed in trunks. Grown over years in a tightly regulated hothouse. Keeping the bloodline pure. Breeding one sturdy tree to another. Finally, the youngest and best seed, given to a trusted friend, passed from one man's hand to another. Kept under glass. Moved to the sunbeam it craves so much after a rainy week. Moved inside. Moved outside. Somebody carrying it here. Somebody else cultivating it there. Somebody else carefully watering the plant. Wiping its leaves. Bringing it out for show when the important people come. Putting it away when the winds blow. Doing everything in their power to ensure it has no strength or hardiness of its own. Doing everything in their power to ensure that should it be neglected it will die. Indeed, if abandoned how will it live? What will it be?

Can you get more human than that, *Maestro*?

It is an absurdity. An anachronism. An orange… alone in the middle of France.

> *She hands him the orange and exits to the house. He watches her go. He has seen her in a new light. He peels the orange.*

VIVALDI   Eaten by a starving Italian composer… in the middle of the night.

> *He begins to hum. He closes his eyes and hums the opening bars of a piece of new piece of music he is composing, as he eats the orange. The music begins… as he imagines it into being.*

Part Four: A Lesson and Nothing More

*VIVALDI crosses to the violin, picks it up and waits for
her. The WOMAN crosses to centre stage where she picks
up and raises the violin slowly and with great ritual as the
piece of music finishes. She plays a simple scale on A and E
strings. No feeling. No care.*

VIVALDI Again.

She does a second one. Frustration shows.

Again.

*She sighs deeply, turns pointedly to him and whips a scale
off angrily. It is better.*

Good.

*She looks at him surprised. A discovery. She goes to play
another. The bell rings. She pauses for a long moment and
goes to play again. The bell rings again and again.
Insistent. Her husband. She finally drops the violin from
her shoulder and holds it out. She doesn't look at him. He
takes it from her. She exits. He stands and stares after her.*

Part Five: A Prayer

*He looks down at his violin. Drunk, maudlin. He speaks to
his violin. Vivaldi's "La Stravaganza: Violin Concerto #4
in A minor." Grave.*

VIVALDI You. I hate you. So merciless and cruel. I've left
you out in the rain so many times… and always some
well-meaning servant manages to rescue you at the last
moment. I've thought about a life without you, and yet,
somehow you always seduce me back… *(sarcastic)* "Most
Highest Grace… I hope and pray that this command may
be that I give you proof of my profound veneration
through the creation of a few poor concertos. Your
humble, devoted and obedient servant…" …and sure
enough here I am teaching scales to a woman married to
one of the most powerful men in France.

And now this is a very dangerous game I play. Time is short. I should be in Vienna—the Emperor—

(to the violin) Are you listening? So now what? I've tried my best to develop this gift you gave me… and yet now somehow I find I've achieved more fame by playing show-pieces for rich people and their friends. The music I write for myself, the music *I* love, can't even pay my bills.

I'm a fraud.

And now, I wait for the end. I can see it on the horizon. I can taste the day when my name will thrill no lady's ear, patron's purse or emperor's fancy. I am out of favour already. Out of style. Out of time. No longer fit to be a priest. No safe haven there. And to be truthful, I couldn't go back even if they would have me. I no longer think of Heaven. Perhaps I will make all their rumours come true and play with the real Devil at my heels.

(to the violin) Perhaps you were here all along.

But… her. She's walking towards the precipice as quickly as I am. If I can make her love the violin, the way she has made me see a garden… is that not a kind of salvation?

> *From behind him, the WOMAN enters with a bouquet of wildflowers. Her face is sad, impassive. Vivaldi's "Concerto #5 in F Major for the Flute." Largo begins.*

❧ MOVEMENT FOUR ❧

Part One: Antea

The WOMAN settles into a pose for a Flora-style portrait for an unseen hired painter. VIVALDI enters and watches her for a moment silently. He decides to play the sycophant. With great energy.

VIVALDI   Ah… Flora.

She starts.

No… please don't let me disturb you. Continue… continue…

*The WOMAN looks at him, then returns to and continues
to hold her position. He walks around her, perilously close.
She watches him with her eyes, trying not to move.*

Silence.

Well… now I see clearly the reason our lesson was
cancelled today.

I suspected you were not really as ill as your lady
attempted to make me believe you were…

*She looks at him. The music ends at the end of the first full
musical phrase. The rest of the scene in silence.*

(laughing) And now I see that I am right…

WOMAN   You do this on purpose don't you?

VIVALDI   *(innocent)* What?

WOMAN   You know I'm trying to sit still.

VIVALDI   You mistake my intentions. I am simply thinking
about the lovely arrangement this painter has made for the
portrait. *(to the painter)* Bravo, sir! Most alluring… Flora.
The Goddess of Love. The Personification of Springtime.
Women's connection to nature, fertility and the wild and
untamed world. Even taking on the attributes of those
fragile flowers she holds so delicately in her hands…

(crossing in close, quietly) And yet you know… many
believe that Flora also represents a courtesan.

What… no response to my taunting?

*The WOMAN smiles despite herself. He has scored
a point. He considers her. A new tactic.*

Are you Flora? A bloom opening to the world for its
pleasure?

WOMAN   *(wryly)* Not exactly.

VIVALDI   Hmmm… perhaps I mistook this arrangement.
Perhaps you are meant to represent Leda… the other
goddess rich women want to be painted as, so badly these

days. The goddess who is ravished by a god in the shape of a swan—

WOMAN   —Or is it their husbands who want them painted that way?

VIVALDI   Good point!

WOMAN   Perhaps these *rich* women should be painted more aptly as Danae... the goddess with the rain of golden coins in her lap.

VIVALDI   *(laughing)* No doubt. I see I have underestimated you. You are a fair opponent in a battle of classical myths. I'm surprised you don't enjoy the opera more...

WOMAN   One can hardly live at Court and not be passably conversant. Like you, I'm fascinated by the connection that the artists of today want to make, between nature and women's bodies.

VIVALDI   Really?

WOMAN   Perhaps you can explain it to me. Nature and goddesses especially. Diana for example. They always seem to depict her as naked and cavorting in the woods with other *women*, when, she really should be hunting for something to eat. Is this really what men wish for most?

VIVALDI   Hmmm... *(laughs)* Yes.

She laughs.

WOMAN   So transparent.

She considers him for a moment.

WOMAN   *(admits)* To be completely honest, I've seen more Floras and Ledas than I care to. My husband loves them. He even has a small private collection of his own.

VIVALDI   Really?

WOMAN   I'm surprised he hasn't shown you. He's very proud of them.

VIVALDI   And this will be added to his collection.

WOMAN   I suppose.

She takes a chance. Silence.

You know, my favourite painting is not a Flora or a Leda. It is in fact, a very small painting, painted by one of your countrymen... Parmigianino. I saw it once at the home of a friend. His portrait of Antea.

He has seen the painting.

VIVALDI   Why your favourite?

She looks at him.

WOMAN   I don't know... she gazes out at you, no clear expression, but somehow he managed to capture a look in her eye. Like an animal that has finally been found after a long hunt. Caught.

VIVALDI   And yet, she lives.

WOMAN   And yet, she lives?

VIVALDI   She is not killed...

WOMAN   No.

VIVALDI   In the painting, she remains in that moment forever. The moment before she is killed.

WOMAN   What else can she do? It is part of the agreement.

VIVALDI   Agreement?

WOMAN   Marriage.

Beat. They both realize what she has said.

VIVALDI   Ah.... Marriage.

Pause.

But what of Antea's husband? What of him? Not a scrap of sympathy for him?

WOMAN   What does he have to do with it?

VIVALDI   *(looking at her)* Imagine his life with her. He can never possess her completely. How can he? Her eyes are so clearly inaccessible. By his fault or another, they remain. Cold. Remote. ...But alluring. We never want the one who

comes to us with their hearts open do we? Her icy smile
and aloof beauty are precisely the qualities that drew him
to her in the first place, that fascinated and intrigued him,
but also those which make her so elusive
in real life.

Pause. She realizes.

WOMAN   You *have* seen the painting.

*She looks at him. Caught. VIVALDI breaks the moment
and goes to leave. Stops.*

VIVALDI   You know… When I saw the painting, *Antea*, I was
most struck by one thing. One thing you didn't mention.

WOMAN   What?

VIVALDI   In that painting… I was struck by the weasel draped
so sensually over her shoulder. Its head lies so warily near
her private area. What could Parmigianino have meant to
symbolize with that I wonder?

Pause. She turns and looks him full in the eyes.

WOMAN   A warning to those who venture too close?

A moment.

VIVALDI   Who knows?

He breaks it.

Same time tomorrow, Your Excellency. This time… bring
your violin.

Touché. He exits. She smiles.

Part Two: A Spell

*VIVALDI alone. He imagines her standing before him with
her violin. He reaches out to touch her. Vivaldi's "Sonata
for Cello and Harpsichord #5 in E minor." Largo.*

*The WOMAN crosses to the violin, picks it up and takes
up the practicing position. VIVALDI touches her as she
silently plays, like in a dream.*

VIVALDI   Magical touching that slender wrist.

> Memories flood back. Happy ones. The tiny wrists of the
> girls as their fingers ran up and down the necks of their
> violins. Music flooding in through open doors and down
> endless hallways. Laughter floating in through the windows
> with the sunlight. Skirts rustling as they ran down the
> stairs out to the vine-covered *conservatorio* piazza...

> Oh the softness of her skin. Delicate. Tender. Outline of my
> fingers on her skin where I gripped her for the correction.
> Map of my touch. My hand almost follows the translucent
> veins tracing down her arm to her bent elbow... leading
> up to her white shoulder—

> So close now, her smell overwhelming. The musky, heady
> smell of her sweat mixed with powder, perfume... cloves
> and cinnamon... sweet and spicy...

Part Three: Practicing

*The dream fades as the music slowly fades out. He is left
staring into space. The WOMAN plays the beginnings of
Vivaldi's "Violin Concerto in A Minor." The Third
Movement, Presto that she will play at the end. Near the
end of the first phrase, she notices him. He isn't paying
attention.*

WOMAN   *Maestro?*

> *He regains himself.*

VIVALDI   I heard you practicing earlier today.

WOMAN   Oh?

VIVALDI   Through the window.

WOMAN   I'm sorry, I should have closed the casement, there
is no need for you, or anyone else, to be subjected to my
mindless meanderings.

VIVALDI   That was exactly what I was going to compliment
you on.

WOMAN   What do you mean?

VIVALDI What were you thinking about when you were practicing?

WOMAN I was… thinking about… I don't know… all sorts of things I suppose. I know I am supposed to play for at least an hour at a time, but it's so difficult to keep concentrating—

VIVALDI —Exactly.

WOMAN I don't understand.

VIVALDI You were daydreaming.

WOMAN I suppose—

VIVALDI —I could hear all those daydreams in your playing.

WOMAN And that's good.

VIVALDI Yes, you were surrendering yourself to the monotony and boredom of practice and there in that tedious place, you were able to stop imposing your general ideas of what you think the piece is about…. Oh this piece is *sad*… or this piece is *happy*…. You were able to find the true heart of the piece itself. And that is, I am happy to say as it was *my étude*, as complex and as varied as your imagination. It transported you somewhere.

Pause. She is lost in her own memory.

WOMAN It was a moment that I remembered. Something I had forgotten about.

He looks at her.

What? It's nothing.

He keeps looking at her.

Honestly…

He takes the bow out of her hand. Stand off. She finally gives in. Reluctant.

I was remembering a time when I was a very little girl. My mother was getting ready to go out to a *masque* ball. Something very important… the house was full of excitement.

She was very, very beautiful, my mother. When I was little, she was the most beautiful woman I had ever seen. Dark hair, pale skin, eyes so dark they were black, and so slight and delicate. As fragile as a bird. I watched all the ladies scurrying about getting her ready. Lacing her up, helping her on with the heavy brocade dress and her most exquisite wig and jewels. And when the final dusting of powder had been blown gently onto her upturned face, the final drops of perfume had been dabbed behind her ears, and in her bosom, just before they put her feathered mask on, somehow in the midst of all that activity, she caught my face, my little face, adoring her in the mirror. And she turned and smiled at me, just at me, her eyes were open and shining. And in that moment she was dazzling. I knew at that moment that I wanted to be her. Just like her.

The memory, which began as a good one, has taken on a darker note by the end.

VIVALDI   It's a lovely memory.

WOMAN   Yes. Well.

VIVALDI   Ah… so it's not just simply a happy memory.

Pause.

WOMAN   It's the only memory I have like that of her. She didn't look at me very often.

VIVALDI   I'm sure she loved you very much, whether she showed you or not.

WOMAN   You surprise me, *Maestro*. I never thought you a sentimentalist. You want to see her in her best light. If I've learned anything through my life, I'm not sure if it's wise to try and repaint the past with the colour of sentimental love. In my experience, that tends to make the present situation somewhat harder to bear.

The simpler truth about my mother is she didn't look at me very often. She didn't look at anyone. She was very alone… I suppose she had other things on her mind.

VIVALDI   Like practicing.

WOMAN   Like the teacher you are, you always try to bring it back to the lesson at hand, don't you, *Maestro*.

VIVALDI   Yes, but hear me out. Being lonely is not a bad thing. It's not a bad thing for a *musician*. The ability to live in loneliness, in our own thoughts as tortured as they may be, is what allows us to practice for as long as it takes to achieve the skills that we strive for. We simply couldn't do it if we weren't able to live in that place day in and day out.

WOMAN   So… if I follow your *treatise* though to its logical end, had my mother been handed a cello, you are proposing that she would rival *you* for fame and fortune?

VIVALDI   *(laughs)* Perhaps.

WOMAN   I see.

VIVALDI   And if I may continue my *treatise*, as you call it, on music, let me just say this. Like the mother you describe, a good composition is not simple and one sided. And like the past, it should never be washed with the *colour of sentimental love* either. A piece of music is as multi-faceted and dimensional as a… …garden. It takes many viewings to truly appreciate and understand. It is alive and it is changing.

> *A moment between them. He hands her the bow. She places the violin on her shoulder and prepares to start again. Pause. A plea.*

WOMAN   Do you really think things can change?

> *Pause.*

VIVALDI   Some days.

> *They can't look at each other.*

(gently) And now… back to practicing.

> *She plays a long drawn out single note. Sweet and sad. She plays it again. Again as she exits. The piece melds into the Largo from Winter, "The Four Seasons."*

Part Four: A Dream

VIVALDI alone. The WOMAN appears part way through.
A statue.

VIVALDI   A dream. She is dressed in a gown of gold. She is at
Versailles. In the Royal Quarters… the suites that no
outsider has seen but architects Louis Le Vau and Ange-
Jacque Gabriel. I hide myself in the shadows and watch as
she steps carefully up the Queen's staircase that leads to
the luscious gilt and blossom-pink suite of rooms. One
wall is covered in tall, ornate glass doors, draped in heavy
embroidered silk. She walks towards them and throws one
set open.

Ah… the light! *The Parterre du Midi*…. The garden.
Adorned with statues and fountains. She is staring at
something… to the west, at the end of the Royal Walk, sits
the Fountain of Apollo. Gold… glorious… bathed in the
light of end of day, the sun god rises in his chariot from
the water. A chariot so full of life, I can feel the tug of the
horses on their bits as it strains to escape into the sky. She
begins to run.

I follow her quickly out onto the *terrasse*… and down the
graceful curve of the staircase to the grounds…. She's so
far ahead. She has already reached the fountain. A distant
figure as she pulls herself onto the thin stone ledge circling
the fountain and without a thought. She leaps… towards
the water… towards what? Freedom. The water breaks
like a slap. I can't seem to see her… I can only imagine her
corset tight like a watery embrace pulling her down.
I want to save her. I can't seem to move… I'm paralyzed….
Whwa! She breaks through the surface… a swirl of silk
and hair and arms…. She fights to move towards the
chariot… but… too late. Apollo leaves without her. She
screams to him as the chariot lifts off but he, like me, can't
seem to hear her cries. I can only watch helplessly like
her… his golden cape fluttering behind him as he travels
up to the beckoning twilight, disappearing in its
darkening embrace.

When I look back down, somehow, she has managed to reach the stone base where the chariot once stood… and pull herself gasping onto it. But as she stands forlornly watching his final ascent… the gold drips off her heavy dress with the water and the dress stiffens where it hangs like ice and she's frozen. She has become a statue. She has replaced him. Amongst the gilded legions of Greek gods and goddesses, she alone stands out. A grey, lone statue of a woman.

Made of stone and looking to heaven.

The piece ends.

Part Five: A Leaf

He exits leaving the WOMAN alone in the garden. The statue come alive. Night. It has become a sad and desolate place.

WOMAN   I'm here, Garden. I'm here to whisper to you…. To pray. To what? To find an answer? No. Much simpler.

A leaf. One fallen leaf. One errant branch. One single pebble out of place. Some sign that something is out of order with this world, something is imperfect, and has been allowed to exist and not eradicated immediately. Please do not confirm my worst fears.

She prays silently for a long moment. She opens her eyes. Nothing has changed.

❧ MOVEMENT FIVE ❧

Part One: A Gift

An evening at the Grand House. VIVALDI enters and stands at the back of the room. The WOMAN watches him for a moment. She comes forward and addresses the guests.

WOMAN   If you would indulge me, I would like to pay tribute to our most honoured guest, *Maestro* Vivaldi, who most unfortunately must be leaving us after a most gracious stay of only a handful of weeks in our house. As you may know, during his time here, he has been attempting to teach me the violin, and I would like to thank him for his most kind tutelage.

VIVALDI is surprised at this public tribute.

You are all, no doubt, most familiar with his exceptional and pleasing *concerti*, one of which he has been composing for my husband these past weeks, and his past works, which we have had the honour of enjoying during his stay here… but I have chosen something more singular and rare for your pleasure this evening.

An aria… from *Maestro* Vivaldi's first opera, *Ottone in Villa*.

A murmur in the crowd. She turns and bows to him. Her gift to him. He accepts the applause of the crowd, stunned. The opening strains of Ottone in Villa *begins and a soprano begins to sing quietly and powerfully. The WOMAN joins VIVALDI. They listen to the opening bars of the aria side by side.*

WOMAN   *(translating the song)*
The shadows, the breeze and the brook
Return the echo of my sorrow.
Are they only here, oh God?
To feel compassion?

Pause.

You wrote that a long time ago.

VIVALDI   Yes.

Pause.

WOMAN   Before you were famous.

VIVALDI   Yes.

Pause.

WOMAN   I marvel at how you could capture my soul so precisely.

Pause.

VIVALDI *(turning to look at her)* Fellow believer.

She turns and looks at him. An understanding. They are in love. The piece ends. Applause. She bows deeply to him. A gift. He accepts the applause of the courtiers.

She exits. As the piece continues, VIVALDI pulls out the composition he was writing earlier and stares at it. He carefully rolls it up and ties it with a ribbon from his wig. He sits for a moment and listens to the aria as it finishes.

Part Two: Goodbye

The WOMAN enters. It is time for him to leave.

WOMAN Your carriages are here.

VIVALDI Ah yes. Your husband has seen to everything.

Pause.

WOMAN There is a great crowd outside to see you off.

VIVALDI nods. A painful silence.

VIVALDI *(quietly to her)* I've gotten one last chance to redeem myself. The Emperor is in Vienna, but he's very sick. He has sent for me. They say, he would like to give me a final commission—

WOMAN —I understand.

They look at each other. Too much. She turns away.

Thank you.

For everything.

Pause.

VIVALDI You are musical, you know? In spite of yourself. You feel the heart of the piece in your soul and it shows in your playing. You have that gift. No one can take that away from you.

He pulls out a scroll, and holds it to her. She reaches to accept it. He doesn't let go.

When you play it, enjoy each note and each moment as it goes by.

He pulls her into him. We think they might kiss, but instead he kisses her gently on the forehead. When she opens her eyes, he's gone. She turns away and opens it. It is a manuscript of a new piece. For her.

WOMAN   Goodbye.

Part Three: Eight Ways to Say Goodbye

VIVALDI alone in the forest.

VIVALDI   Eight ways to say goodbye:

Find Emperor Charles dead in Vienna before he's signed your final commission. Sell twenty concertos to the *Ospedale Della Pieta* for a ducat apiece when they're really worth a hundred. Send a letter to every wealthy patron you know. Beg for money. Starve. Die alone. Bury yourself in a pauper's grave with no marker.

Silence.

Be forgotten for two hundred years.

Part Four: The Precipice

The WOMAN alone in the forest.

WOMAN   On one side the precipice. I can fail. He's sitting out there wanting me to fail. The final humiliation. So he can excuse his bad behaviour when he finally eliminates me from his life. So he won't feel so bad when he says goodbye.

The other side…

She can't finish that thought.

Part Five: The Final Movement

The WOMAN takes the violin and enters the court, in front of her husband. Everyone.

WOMAN   Eight ways to say goodbye...

Play badly. Play well. Humiliate yourself. Exonerate yourself. Prove something to him. Prove something to yourself.

See the world in a different way...

She raises the violin. She begins to play. Vivaldi's "Violin Concerto in A Minor." The third movement Presto. It is timid. Destined to fail. She crumbles to a complete stop. She looks out at the audience, the court, him...

Slowly, as if from Heaven, a single leaf falls. Something changes. She plays.

It is glorious.

The End.

photo by Sandy Spear

Mieko Ouchi works as a writer, actor and director in theatre, film and TV. A graduate of the University of Alberta's BFA Acting program, she has been working professionally across Canada since 1992. *The Red Priest (Eight Ways to Say Goodbye)*, her first full-length play, has been produced across the country, and was nominated for a Governor General's Literary Award in 2004, winning the Carol Bolt Prize from the Canadian Authors Association in 2005. *The Blue Light*, her second play, won the Betty Mitchell Award for Best New Play in 2007. Her award winning films "Shepherd's Pie and Sushi," "By This Parting," "Samurai Swing" and "Minor Keys" have played at more than 30 film festivals across North America and aired on the CBC, W Network, Bravo! and DUTV in Philadelphia. She is the Artistic Co-Director of Concrete Theatre, a theatre for young audiences. Mieko was the recipient of a Queen's Golden Jubilee Medal in 2003 for her contribution to the arts. She lives and works in Edmonton.